Contents

Introduction

In my ABC of Fruit Growing I have endeavoured to provide reliable information, all of which is based on personal experience. If I have omitted a fruit from the list it simply means that I have not grown it. In every case my variety lists are far from complete and this I regret, but perhaps my comments on a particular variety may differ from reports previously published. Tastes also differ, as do soils and districts.

I was privileged to grow up in a fruit growing district and was always able to enjoy fresh fruit from our own orchard; my earliest memories are of nests of Williams' pears ripening in newly erected haystacks. I used to pick the pears green and lay them in the freshly dried hay in the stack, the heat of which was just right to bring the pears up to ripening perfection. I remember, too, the large Blenheim Orange apple trees and, luckily, the not too frequent falls from a ladder with overladen baskets of fruit; also the aroma of tons of strawberries as the nightly fruit trains from Wisbech went their way to the markets in the north.

What a change has taken place since then, gone are the days when haystacks got so hot that not infrequently they caught fire. When fruit trees were so tall that ladders were needed at fruit picking time and fruit specials puffed their way from Wisbech each evening during the summer.

My fruit growing experience started on a fertile soil in the Isle of Ely, continued for thirty years with 18 hectares (45 acres) of fruit on the heaviest clay soils in Nottinghamshire and since 1967 has been at Clack's Farm in Worcestershire.

I believe that every gardener in this country could grow some fruit, a large garden is not necessarily a pre-requisite, all that is needed is the will and I would like to think that this book will help. As in other forms of gardening, the wise fruit grower plants a wide range of subjects rather than a lot of one particular type of fruit, there is nothing worse than a glut of unwanted windfall apples in a garden devoid of other fruits.

With strawberries, raspberries and other soft fruits so easy to grow, there is no reason why a small fruit garden should not provide a family with home-grown fruit throughout the whole year. Indulge in the fun of forcing strawberries; a strawberry season can start towards the end of June and carry on until the frosts come in November. Raspberries can also have a long picking season, from July until November, it is all a question of planting the right varieties. Both raspberries and strawberries can be frozen for use during the out-of-

Arthur Billitt's
ABC of Fruit Growing

Hamlyn
London · New York · Sydney · Toronto

Acknowledgements

Line drawings by Val Biro
Pat Brindley and The Harry Smith Horticultural Photographic
Collection for supplying colour photographs

First published in 1979 by
The Hamlyn Publishing Group Limited
London · New York · Sydney · Toronto
Astronaut House, Feltham, Middlesex, England

Some material in this book has already
been published in *Amateur Gardening* magazine

Filmset in England by Photocomp Ltd., Birmingham
in 11 on 12pt Plantin.
Printed in Italy.

ISBN 0 600 33696 4

season period, we are never without either. Some examples of varieties for the very small garden might be helpful: raspberries: Malling Jewel for summer fruiting and Heritage for the autumn; strawberries: Tamella for summer fruiting and Gento for autumn fruiting; and as few as twenty plants of a variety are well worth growing.

Thinking of limited space problems, I would stress the importance of rootstocks. Apples are now grafted or budded on dwarfing rootstocks and fruit picking from a ladder is now a thing of the past. Much of the research work on fruit-tree rootstocks has been done in the UK and we should all be grateful for the dedication of the East Malling Research Station staff. Their successes followed by practical recommendations have made it possible for tree fruit growing to be worthwhile even in very small gardens. So don't just order or ask for an apple tree. Do make sure that the variety of your choice is on a dwarfing rootstock.

Throughout the ABC my choice of varieties has been based on quality, unless a variety has flavour as a natural attribute no cultural techniques however good can put it there; all that can be achieved is some improvement.

The recent development and events in fruit growing have all occurred with the interests of commercial fruit growing as the objective; we, the amateur fruit growers, are benefiting from the spin-off. As regards growing techniques we may share the same objectives to a certain extent but when it comes to fruit quality the amateurs' objectives differ dramatically. Commercial fruit growing is concerned with yield, travel qualities, appearance, shelf life and profitability; flavour is way down on the list. For me flavour is all important; unless a variety has a built-in quality fruit flavour I refuse to give it space in our garden. However, I am always prepared to give new varieties a trial before expressing an opinion. Fruit trees, soft fruit canes and strawberry plants are all expensive these days, and my advice is place your orders in good time with a reliable nursery.

I am a great believer in gardening for health, the exercise is good when taken in regular doses and fresh home-grown fruit with its vitamin C content must be good for all of us. The adage 'an apple a day keeps the doctor away' is not too far from the truth, at least that has been my experience. All that remains for me to say is 'do enjoy your fruit growing' it will be good for you and your family.

Climate and Soil

Wherever it is proposed to plant fruit the local climatic conditions must be taken into consideration. Altitude, wind, rainfall, amount of sunshine, temperature ranges and geographical location are all important factors.

Climate, its effect on growing fruit

Sites more than 180 m (600 ft) above sea level are usually unsuitable for tree fruits except maybe for cider apples or very hardy culinary varieties. A south or west hillside site at a much lower altitude could have advantages over a place situated in the valley below, which would be far more subject to spring-frost damage due to the downward flow of cold air. Exposed positions subject to heavy winds are unsuitable for tree fruits; pears especially suffer foliage damage very easily. Windbreaks can be erected or planted to mitigate the problem, but even so in locations within 7 km (5 miles) of the coast the salt-laden inshore winds still make tree fruit growing difficult. The amount of annual rainfall and the time it occurs are important – there are only a few areas in the country with a rainfall below 60 cm (24 in) a year, the amount that is regarded as just about right for growing fruit. However, it may be necessary to resort to artificial watering during the spring and summer for best results. In areas of high rainfall the problems are different; dessert varieties of apples such as Cox's Orange Pippin become more difficult to grow well enough to produce a good quality crop and it is wiser to plant varieties known to do well in the district. Diseases such as apple and pear scab are more troublesome in the wetter districts, especially when the rainfall is coupled with high temperatures.

For quality dessert apples, pears and plums, summer sunshine and warmth are needed. Apples are generally more tolerant of cold than pears; only the south-eastern corner of the country has sunshine records and temperatures high enough to grow the best varieties of pears really well. In less favoured districts it is better to be less ambitious with regard to varieties, a check on local successes is always wise before embarking on a planting scheme.

Apricots, peaches and nectarines all need more sunshine than we normally have in this country, so it is only by planting them in front of south- or west-facing walls or fences, and by providing some form of protection against spring frosts that we can hope to beat our climate even in the southern half of the country. Raspberries and most other cane fruits love the cooler growing conditions of Scotland, where some of the best quality raspberries are grown. Strawberries, too, will grow almost anywhere in the country, the limiting factor in the wetter districts is botrytis (grey mould), a disease which causes the fruit to rot. Again the choice of less susceptible varieties will help overcome the problem.

Frost damage

Apart from such unusual happenings as bark splitting during exceptionally severe winters, all our fruit trees are able to withstand the rigours of the winter; it is the spring frosts that cause concern. It is the damage done to fruit buds just prior to bud break and the growth stages onwards until the end of May that worry fruit growers. A single night's frost can severely reduce the crop or, at worst, entirely eliminate it. In the build-up to a spring frost the colder air flows downwards, consequently fruit blossoms on trees on a hillside may escape damage, whilst the same varieties of fruit trees lower down in the valley may have their blossoms ruined. Although the blossom may still look beautiful the next morning, frosts of just a few degrees can destroy the essential parts of the flowers to such an extent that fruit set does not follow. If frosts occur after fruit set they can kill the fruitlets or, at the very least, cause russeting and cracking.

Opposite: succulent strawberries (see page 75)

Before embarking on a fruit tree planting programme it is wise to establish whether or not your garden is a high or low risk location for spring frosts. For those in a high risk location it is sensible to select varieties known to be less susceptible to frost damage, for example the apple Charles Ross has been known to come through unscathed while Cox's Orange Pippin and others have been wiped out.

Something on the same line could be said of soft fruit, for instance in two recent years the blackcurrant Jet was the only variety in my garden that escaped some frost damage, it may not be more resistant but it flowers a lot later than most other varieties.

It is possible sometimes to reduce spring frost damage by simply making a sizeable opening at ground level at the lowest end of the fruit garden to provide the cold air with a means of escape. It is in areas where the cold air builds up that the temperatures are lowest and frost damage is greatest. Continuous overhead spraying of the trees with water during the night prevents frost damage, and this method is used in many commercial orchards.

Soil types

The first requirement of the soil for fruit growing is good drainage. On light and gravelly soils this will be naturally good, on medium soils overlying gravel or rock it will probably be satisfactory. It is on the heavier soil types overlying clay or chalk that problems may occur. The ideal soil types for fruit growing lie within the medium soil ranges where the top soil is deep; the natural fertility is then likely to be good and with such an advantage it is not difficult to enrich and maintain the soil at a higher level if it need be. Light and gravelly soils are naturally hungry and plant nutrients are quickly leached away well beyond the reach of the roots of even quite large trees. On such soils the regular surface applications of organic material such as well-rotted compost or manure may be the

only way of holding the fertilisers where they are needed to prevent starvation symptoms developing as the trees grow older.

Pest problems, particularly red spider mite, are usually more troublesome on light gravelly soils, especially in areas of low rainfall. Heavier soils, especially those overlying chalk or calcareous sub-soils, can present nutritional difficulties when growing apples or pears but less so for stone fruits. This subject is dealt with under trace elements in the chapter on fertilisers.

Drainage

Whilst soil moisture is essential for tree growth, stagnant water in the ground (water that is unable to drain away) can be fatal. For successful fruit growing the land drainage needs to be satisfactory, in other words during periods of heavy rainfall the water must be able to get away. Trees standing in ground subject to waterlogging for even short periods can suffer from serious root die back. Additionally on heavy, poorly-drained soils, other problems such as canker develop. The canker which eats into the wood of the trees, particularly apples, can be treated, but only by improving the drainage will the cause of the trouble be alleviated. Drainage problems occur on the heavier soils especially those overlying clay; fortunately the lighter and medium soil types, often over gravel or open freer-draining sub-soils, present lesser drainage problems.

When large areas require improved drainage the task is relatively simple provided the necessary outlets for the surplus water can be provided. Agricultural land drains laid in lines at distances related to the nature of the soil are the answer, but in the small garden where the territory beyond the fence is out of bounds, the problem may not be so straight forward. It is useless to lay either drainage pipes or underground clinker tracks if the water gathered is unable to get away. Neither is there any good purpose served by digging out planting holes and filling in with a lighter soil, the fact that the water in the soil will still be stagnant is the real problem.

Opposite: an enviable crop of pears (see page 68)

A continual excess of water in the soil leads to poor growth above and below ground and whilst the water is there the root action will be insufficient to correct the situation.

Soft fruit can be grown on raised ridges so that their roots do not stand in water; the same type of approach in difficult situations can be applied to tree fruits but in both cases it can only be an attempt to make the best of a growing medium that is not really suitable for fruit growing.

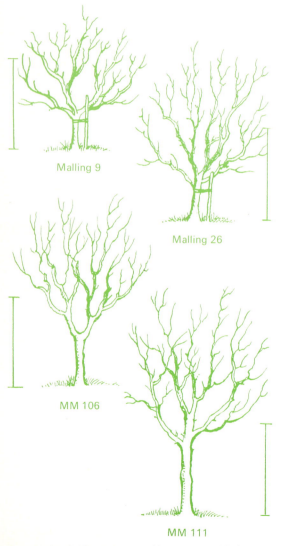

Rootstocks of different vigour effect the overall habit of an apple tree

Choosing your Tree

Gone are the days when we simply order a fruit tree, name the variety and hope that all will eventually turn out alright, whether we grow the tree as a cordon, a small bush, a half standard or even a full standard. The variety, of course, is important but the rootstock on which it was grafted or budded will determine whether or not it will behave as we would wish.

Rootstocks
So much research and development has gone into the selection of rootstocks for particular uses that I regard the inclusion of the rootstock type on the label at the time of sale as being just as important as the name of the variety. It is the only safeguard we have against buying trees with built-in growth habits that conflict with our wishes. I am pleased to say that some suppliers are already co-operating by labelling every tree with both the variety and the rootstock details. For the garden fruit grower there are four apple rootstocks which should cover his needs.

Malling 9 is a dwarfing rootstock, suitable for closely-planted trees on good soils. It is the one I would recommend for cordons or small bush trees. The roots are fibrous and brittle and consequently anchorage is very poor and therefore the trees must have support for the whole of their lives. Malling 9 brings the tree into cropping early and the fruit is always large for the variety.

Malling 26 is slightly more vigorous and could replace Malling 9 for planting on lighter soils, it too requires permanent support.

MM 106 is a semi-dwarfing rootstock, bred for its resistance to woolly aphid; especially suitable for bush trees and espaliers.

MM 111 is a vigorous rootstock also bred for its resistance to woolly aphid; especially suit-

able for half-standard or full-standard trees.
Malling 7 is a rootstock I would avoid, it is sometimes sold as a dwarfing rootstock, but in my experience it has proved difficult to manage, producing far too much whippy growth and little fruit.

Average planting distances on good soils, bush trees on Malling 9: 4 m (13 ft), on Malling 26: 5·5 m (18 ft), on MM 106: 6 m (20 ft), half-standard and full-standard trees on MM 111: 7 m (23 ft). Closer planting could be practical on less fertile soils or when planting weak-growing varieties.

There are two well proven rootstocks for pears: Quince A and Quince C.
Quince A is semi-vigorous, therefore makes a sizeable tree. It usually takes a few seasons before coming into full cropping.
Quince C is semi-dwarfing, therefore more suitable for garden use where space may be limited, certainly the right choice for cordon pears. Bush trees on Quince C must be kept staked throughout their cropping lives.

For plums there is a choice of several rootstocks.
St Julien A which is semi-dwarfing and is the one I would recommend for any form of trained plums, I also favour it for bush trees.
St Julien Seedling is more vigorous than St Julien A and is useful for planting on poorish soils.
Myrobalan is a vigorous rootstock that is commonly used for damsons which are by nature not very vigorous.
Colt is a new dwarfing rootstock for sweet cherries.
F 12.1 is a vigorous rootstock more suitable for the weaker growing Morello cherry.

Maiden trees

I am a great believer in planting one-year-old trees (maidens), not only are they cheaper to buy but the long term results are better. Maiden trees seldom show any signs of transplanting shock, the vigour of youth is there, the root system is smaller and therefore less likely to have been damaged by lifting from the nursery. Whereas in past years a transplanting shock to a three-year-old tree was considered desirable to bring the tree into fruiting, nowadays, with the universal use of modern dwarfing rootstocks, apples and pears come into bearing almost immediately. By starting with a maiden tree the training is more flexible and the tree can be shaped to suit your needs.

Cordon fruit

Tree fruits grown on a single stem are called cordons. By planting these close together it is possible to grow a considerable number of different fruits in a much wider range of varieties in a small area than by using any other method. Apples are ideal subjects for this treatment, I plant one-year-old (maidens) trees on the Malling, rootstock at 1 m (3 ft) apart, sloping the trees at an angle of 45°. The dwarfing rootstock limits the vigour and growth of the tree throughout its life; in addition the fact that the stem of the tree is always at a sloping angle slows down the sap flow. This combination of growth controls results in an abundance of fruit bud development whilst at the same time the wood growth is less prolific.

Planting on a more vigorous rootstock than Malling 9 can present problems after two or three years when the tree has become fully established. I know the arguments in favour of MM 106 rootstock, it looks a better tree at time of purchase but when it gets going it can be too strong a grower to be kept in check as a cordon. On any soil I prefer to plant on Malling 9 and from then on I can be in complete control of tree growth, on soils of low fertility it is only a question of extra feeding to compensate for the differences.

For support strong posts are needed (I use stout angled iron), 45 cm (18 in) in the ground and 1·5 m (5 ft) out of the ground, to carry three strands of strong round galvanised wire at equal distances apart. With the posts and wires in position I then tie in 2 m (6 ft) canes, this time using thin wire, placing them 1 m (3 ft) apart and sloping at an angle 45° away from the sun. The use of canes makes for rigid support of the single stems which are tied to the canes with soft fillis string.

A cordon-trained fruit tree

Summer pruning
of a cordon

Winter pruning of a cordon

Tip-bearing varieties such as Worcester Pearmain are not suitable for growing as cordons as the pruning necessary to maintain the single stem tree removes most of the fruit buds. Pruning of cordon apples is done twice a year, once in late July or early August when the new growths are shortened to 4 or 5 leaf buds and then again during the dormant season in winter when further cutting back of the summer-pruned wood to fruit buds, plus thinning out of surplus growths may be necessary. Avoid too-early summer pruning and never allow them to become more like bush trees than cordons. Pruning back to within 15 or 20 cm (6 or 8 in) of the main stem each winter is essential, done carefully sufficient fruit buds will be left for the following season's crop. Cordon-grown apples are usually first quality fruit, colour and size are often better than those on bush trees, pest and disease control is easier and can be more effective.

Pears can be grown as cordons and planting distances are the same as for apples. There is, however, less choice of suitable rootstocks, Quince C is a semi-dwarfing rootstock and virus-free stock is now available, it is the rootstock I would recommend as it is not only less vigorous than Quince A but comes into bearing much more quickly after planting.

Pears generally do not take kindly to hard and regular pruning, some varieties dislike it more than others. Williams' Bon Chrétien, Conference, Onward and Doyenné du Comice are four that I have been able to crop fairly consistently when growing them as cordons.

Red and white currants and gooseberries are excellent subjects for growing as cordons and again the technique is basically the same. It is best to start with one-year-old plants or cuttings for training up the sloping canes. They all crop freely on old wood so the shortening of the lateral growths each year not only maintains the cordon shape but also ensures fruiting from top to bottom of the plant. Blackcurrants are not suitable for growing as cordons as they crop on the previous year's wood.

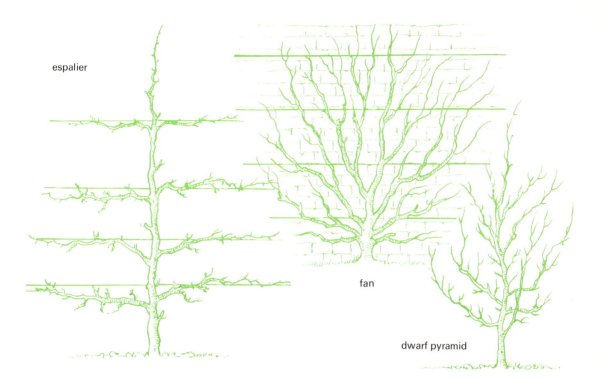

espalier

fan

dwarf pyramid

Trained fruit

In addition to the training of apples and pears as cordons, other methods of training can also make it possible to grow high quality fruit in a relatively small area, provided it is an open site and gets plenty of sunshine. In full shade fruit trees survive but with exceptions, such as Morello cherries and Victoria plums, cannot be expected to give very satisfactory cropping results.

Both apples and pears can be trained as dwarf pyramids, planted upright at 1·25 m (4 ft) apart the trees are staked and tied individually. The laterals are pruned to form a pyramid with a base of about 1 m (3 ft). If more than one row is planted the space between the rows should be at least 2 m (6 ft) to allow room for operations such as pruning, spraying and picking. On the best soils I suggest planting apples on either Malling 9 or Malling 26 rootstocks, on less fertile soils MM 106 rootstock should be used. I would plant pears on Quince C rootstock.

For an attractive fruit-growing feature it is difficult to equal a well-grown espalier tree with its branches trained horizontally on either side of the main stem. Trees trained on post and wire fencing can provide an attractive division screen and at the same time produce the highest quality fruit. High walls or fences also provide opportunities but horizontal support wires should be fixed about 15 cm (6 in) in front of the wall or fence and kept taut by using long metal vine eyes for the job. On espaliers each horizontal branch is spur pruned, which rules out the use of tip-bearing varieties. For espalier-trained apples I would plant on MM 106 rootstock and pears on Quince A.

Fan training on a wall or fence is well suited to peaches, nectarines, plums and cherries, a space of at least 4 m (13 ft) is needed for each tree. Again the horizontal support wires should be fixed 15 cm (6 in) in front of the wall or fence. It is wise to buy trees that have been already started as fan-trained trees in the nursery and to build up the fan-type extension growths gradually afterwards. In this country fan training is the only practical approach to growing peaches and nectarines outside, free-standing trees have been tried but seldom with continuing success. If possible I would choose

St Julien A rootstock for peaches, nectarines and plums; for sweet cherries the new semi-dwarfing rootstock Colt, whilst for Morello cherries it would be rootstock F 12.1.

Family trees

These are sometimes called 'every man's orchard' as each tree produces three different varieties of either apples or pears. The family trees, which are available as bush trees on 60 cm to 1 m (2 to 3 ft) stems, provide the answer to the pollination problem in a small garden.

By planting a single tree on which are grafted three carefully matched varieties, the blossoming occurs simultaneously, growth behaviour is balanced and cropping of all three varieties becomes a regular feature. There are five different combinations of apple varieties to choose from but only one selection of pear varieties: Williams' Bon Chrétien, Conference and Doyenné du Comice – which in any case would be my choice.

Three pears on one tree:
left, Conference, top, Doyenné du Comice and bottom, Williams' Bon Chrétien

Planting and Growing

Before going out and buying your fruit trees and bushes decide where you are going to plant them, and then prepare the ground well in advance.

Planting

I prefer to plant both trees and cane fruits during the fully dormant season from November to February and the earlier the better. Early November is ideal if the soil is in good condition because when planted at this time they start to make new roots almost immediately.

Careful planting results in quick establishment; each hole should be prepared in advance and should be large enough to take the roots without cramping and just deep enough so the plant is at exactly the same depth as it was in the nursery. First drive in the supporting stake and then, with the roots well spread out in the hole, the first covering should be with the finest sieved soil available. After a check to make sure that there are no air spaces between the roots, apply a scattering of bone meal and continue filling, making sure that the soil is firmed with the boot as you go.

Container-grown trees and cane fruits can be planted during the growing season but I would not recommend it as a general practice.

Soil sickness

Soil sickness problems are only likely to occur when trees or soft fruits are planted on land which has recently grown fruit. So if fruit of any kind is planted on fresh ground or ground that has had a rest for several years it is unlikely to be a problem.

I have been able to replant successfully strawberries and raspberries on the same ground by incorporating a considerable quantity of well-rotted compost when preparing

16

Planting a fruit tree

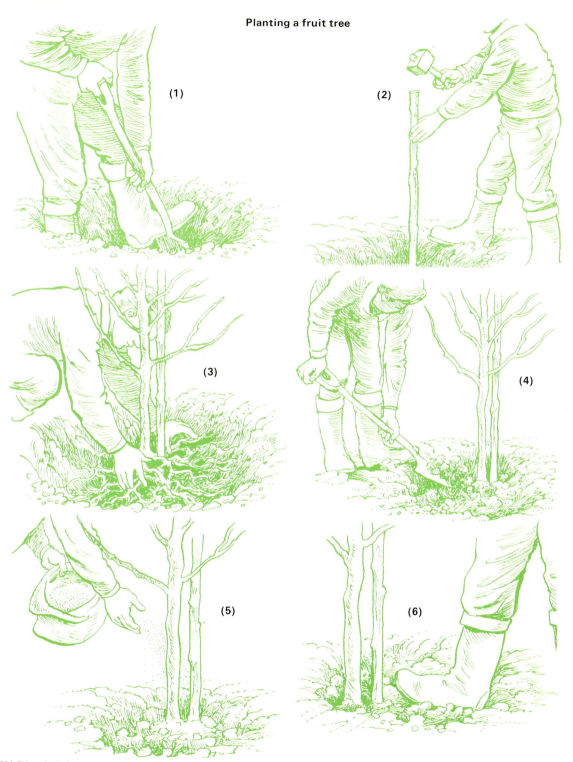

(1) Dig a hole large enough to take the full spread of the roots. **(2)** Bang in the supporting stake. **(3)** Spread out the roots of the tree. **(4)** Begin to fill in the hole. **(5)** Sprinkle in some bonemeal as the hole is filled. **(6)** Firm the soil with the boot to make sure there are no air spaces left

17

the land. In the case of replanting fruit trees, the new trees should never be sited in exactly the same positions, the further they are planted away from where the old trees were grubbed out the better; again some well-rotted compost worked into the replanting area will help.

Soil sickness is not fully understood but the adverse effects on the replanted subjects may be due to toxins excreted by the previous crop or to the soil deficiencies built up gradually during the life of the previous crop, which in the case of fruit trees may have extended over many years.

Chemical soil sterilisation can be used to overcome soil sickness. The chemical dazomet has been used successfully prior to replanting strawberries, raspberries and other soft fruits. No doubt it could also be used on ground intended for replanting with fruit trees but the depth of incorporation necessary for complete success might present a problem in itself.

Mulching
The purpose of mulching is to conserve soil moisture and to keep surface-feeding roots cool. This means that a mulch should only be applied when the soil is damp otherwise the mulch has the reverse effect by acting as an umbrella and prevents moisture reaching the roots. Cane fruits, in particular, respond well to an annual late-winter or early-spring mulch but the compost or manure must be well rotted otherwise the young canes' growths may be adversely affected. Partially-rotted compost or manure can cause a nitrogen deficiency due to the demands of the soil bacteria in their quest for nitrogen which they use to complete the rotting-down processes. A thin layer of mulch is best, one thick enough to hold the moisture in without preventing air penetration is ideal, a mulch of this sort can also suppress weeds.

Grassing
It is often more practicable to grow fruit trees in grass but it is never wise to start young fruit trees off with their roots covered with grass. For the first three years all kinds of fruit

Apply a mulch of well-rotted manure or compost around cane fruit in early spring when the soil is damp

Keep a large circle of cultivated soil round young trees to help them get off to a good start

should be given the opportunity to settle down in clean cultivated ground, even if the cultivated area is restricted to a large circle at least 1 m (3 ft) in diameter around each tree. In cultivated ground establishment is quicker and growth is stronger. Apple trees can be grassed down after three years but pears, plums and other tree fruits do much better with clean cultivated land underneath them throughout their cropping lives.

When the time comes to grass down it is best to operate a 'tumble down', which simply means allowing the natural grasses to take over. Weeds will grow as well but these will largely disappear when the grass is cut regularly; the natural grasses, especially annual meadow grass, have shallow root systems and are very suitable for the purpose. Generally speaking fruit colour is better when the trees are growing in grass but more nitrogen and

Hoe round soft fruit bushes to keep ground free of weeds taking care not to damage roots just below the soil surface

water is needed to maintain the production of new woody growth.

Weed control

Weed competition is best kept down to a minimum, weeds compete for moisture, nutrients, light and air and must therefore be regarded as unwanted in the fruit garden.

With soft fruits it is important to start with clean land, the presence of perennial weed roots at the time of planting can only spell trouble and a lot of frustrating effort afterwards. It is much better to spend a whole season cleaning the ground, getting rid of the couch grass and nettles before embarking on a planting programme. A crop of potatoes involves quite a number of movements of the soil and can effectively clean the dirtiest of sites in a single season.

Starting with the soft-fruit garden clean is one thing, keeping it that way is another. A frequent run through with a hoe will prevent germinating weed seedlings from growing up into strong weed plants, the old addage 'one year's seedlings means seven years weeding' is still true – never allow weeds to seed is a good maxim. All soft fruits develop feeding roots close to the surface so it is very important not to disturb them. Surface hoeing is effective without risk of damage to the roots, on the other hand digging near the plants is bound to cause damage.

In a small garden area I would always advocate hoeing as an effective means of weed control rather than the use of chemicals, the latter can be used but considerable care is needed especially if the crops are in small units and varied.

Pollination

When purchasing fruit trees it is important to consider the question of pollination, some varieties are self-fertile but others may need the presence nearby of another variety or even two other varieties which will blossom at the same time. As all of our fruits are by nature merely vehicles for the production and distribution of seed, it is essential for fertilisation of the open blossom to take place.

Cross pollination, the transfer of viable pollen from flower to flower, is accomplished in several ways; by bees which industriously cover vast numbers of flowers over a wide area; by pollinating insects which move more slowly from flower to flower or by the wind which is often the major contributor to a good fruit set. In every case for effective fertilisation some warmth is needed otherwise the pollen will not be viable, hence the fruit-growers wish for fine sunny days at blossom time.

Some varieties are self-fertile and therefore able to set fruit without another partner, nevertheless even these self-sufficient varieties usually crop more consistently when the blossom is fertilised with pollen from another variety. So make sure there are other trees in the area and if possible find out what variety they are or when they flower. Otherwise buy at least two trees which flower at the same time or a family tree to ensure cross pollination can take place.

Containers for fruit growing

Some of the finest fruit I have ever tasted was picked from trees and plants growing with their roots restricted. There is no end to the possibilities, growing fruit in containers opens up avenues not only for the would-be gardener who has no suitable ground or adequate space but also for the gardener who wishes to have fruits not usually happy in our temperate climate.

The containers may be made of various materials, from plastic to wood or concrete. Whatever the material, the first essential is provision for drainage, in other words holes in the bottom so that surplus water can drain away. Stagnant water in a container spells death to the roots. If containers made of soft wood are used it is advisable to treat the wood inside and out with a horticulturally-safe wood preservative before the containers are put into service. Size of container should, of course, be related to the size of the plant to be grown in it, I have used 60-cm (2-ft) square wooden containers with a depth of 60 cm (2 ft) for successfully growing apples and pears over a period of several seasons. I have also fruited apples and pears in 25-cm (10-in) pots but it is better to give them more root space if you wish for continuing success.

Whatever the container it is important to make sure that there is a clear space underneath the drainage holes to allow for effective drainage and to deny earthworms direct entry into the container. Before filling either large or small containers, pieces of broken pot or tiles should be laid roughly over the drainage holes to prevent the compost blocking them.

Whilst peat-based composts can be used for strawberries and other relatively short-stay plants in containers, it is better to use traditional loam-based composts such as John Innes No. 2 for tree and cane fruits. For container growing of fruit trees I would use Malling 9 rootstock for apples and Quince C rootstock for pears; as always I would start with one-year-old trees.

The basic fruit-growing rules apply: the fruit trees or plants will need sunshine, so an open situation is desirable but the natural rainfall will be insufficient to meet their needs and regular watering during the growing season will be essential. To maintain healthy growth it will be necessary to apply a liquid fertiliser with a high-potash content from time to time.

As far as I know there are no exceptions; all our popular fruits can be grown in this way. Container growing is ideal for the patio or backyard fruit grower. For the fruit that are not completely at home in our climate, such as peaches, nectarines, apricots and figs, portable containers make it possible to give the plants the benefit of our summer plus the protection indoors against the severity of the winter and the chance to escape from damaging spring frosts.

Topdressing with fresh potting compost will be needed each year. After several years in a container it may be advisable to lift a tree or bush out of its container completely during the dormant season, trim the roots and replant using fresh potting compost.

Propagation

Fruit trees are propagated either by budding or grafting the selected variety onto the correct rootstock for the situation.

Budding

Whereas in grafting a scion with several buds is used, for budding only a single bud is required to be inserted on to each fruit-tree rootstock. For this reason budding is more generally practised in commercial-fruit-tree production. To be successful some considerable care and expertise is needed. The budding wood should be taken from the tree sometime during the period July to August, the wood buds must be plump at the time. The skill comes in first with the preparation of the rootstock, this means making a 2·5-cm-(1-in-) long down cut followed by a 1-cm-($\frac{1}{2}$-in-) transverse cut in the bark with a sharp budding knife.

More expertise is required for the preparation of the bud as the piece of wood behind the bud has to be removed without damaging or removing the root of the bud. Immediately after preparation the bud is slipped into the incision on the rootstock, the handle of a budding knife being used to lift the bark. With the bud well sealed and the bark back in position the cuts are weatherproof and firmly held in place with a special plastic tape. Timing is extremely important, too-early budding may result in the buds breaking into growth before the winter and this is not desirable.

Grafting

Whereas budding is now generally employed for working fruit on rootstocks, grafting is still the standard method used when it is desirable to overwork an established tree (that is to effect a complete change of variety) or add another variety, maybe for pollination purposes. For grafting, scions are prepared by taking shoots from the current-season's ripened wood after

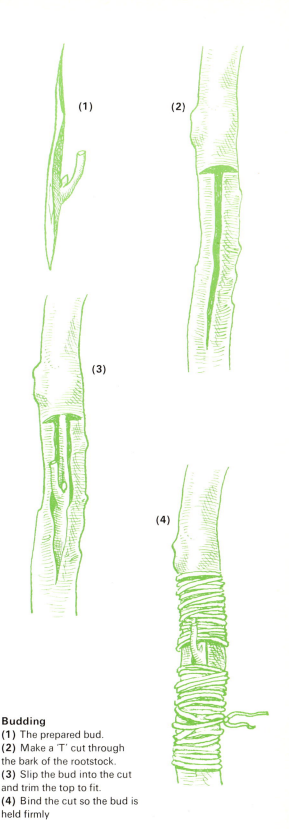

(1)

(2)

(3)

(4)

Budding
(1) The prepared bud.
(2) Make a 'T' cut through the bark of the rootstock.
(3) Slip the bud into the cut and trim the top to fit.
(4) Bind the cut so the bud is held firmly

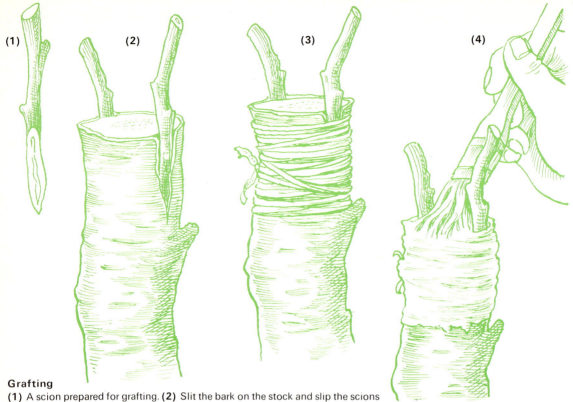

Grafting
(1) A scion prepared for grafting. (2) Slit the bark on the stock and slip the scions into place. (3) Bind the graft so the scions are held firmly. (4) Cover the binding and the end of the branch with grafting wax

leaf fall in the autumn, and storing these without breaking dormancy, heeling them in in full shade.

To overwork completely an established tree the main branches can be cut back in January to within about 60 cm (2 ft) of the trunk. Few minor branches should be left for the time being and cut out later after the scions have taken. April is about the best time for the actual grafting as the sap is then beginning to rise. The first part of the operation consists of making a clean saw cut to remove about 5 cm (2 in) of the cut back branch, followed by a final trimming with a sharp knife. The bark is then cut downwards with the knife point, making a slit of about 8 cm (3 in) long right down to the hard wood, ready to receive the scion. The prepared scion should have a 5-cm (2-in) sloping cut at the bottom end. All is then ready and the cut bark can be lifted carefully at the top end, with the handle of a budding knife, for the insertion of the scion.

If the branch is more than 10 cm (4 in) in diameter it would be advisable to put two scions on, one on either side. When the scion is well seated it should be tied in with raffia and the whole surface, branch end included, covered with grafting wax. For the addition of another variety for pollination purposes the timing and method is the same, the scion or scions may be inserted into a branch, preferably in an open part of the tree.

Seed-raised fruit

There is a fascination in growing fruit from seed but the chances of an outstanding success are very remote even when the hybridisation is expertly carried out – many of us have been lured on by the knowledge that Cox's Orange Pippin was a chance seedling. No varieties of fruit come true from seed, every seedling is an individual with its own character, faults and failings. I would never recommend fruit growing from seed except for fun; there have been too many disappointments especially with seed collected in warmer climates.

Pruning

Pruning fruit trees is not an exact science, in commercial fruit growing so much depends on the way it is done and every fruit grower prunes in the light of experience but will still treat each tree as an individual.

In the fruit garden cropping prospects are so often ruined by the trees being treated as ornamentals and shaped like them by snipping here and there with a pair of secateurs or by drastically cutting them back to restrict their size. Both approaches are wrong; continually trimming a tree results in a tight mass of wood growth and very little fruit, while on the other hand drastic pruning only urges the tree to make more and still more wood growth without fruit buds.

In the case of newly planted trees the first pruning decides the future shape; for instance, a one-year-old tree with its single stem cut back in the winter at say 1 m (3 ft) will eventually make a bush tree on a 60 cm (2 ft) stem (or thereabout). Two-year or older trees will already have made a framework of branches, shortening the branches after planting encourages a further build-up of the branch framework.

The pruning cuts should be carefully placed, as the position of the bud immediately below the cut determines the direction in which the wood growth will develop. From the beginning pruning should be designed to keep the centre of the tree open, so that light and air reaches all the fruit within the tree. Pruning of apples and pears is best done during the winter. Summer pruning of trained trees should be delayed until August as too early pruning results in the fruit buds breaking into growth.

(1) (2) (3) (4)

Pruning to form an open-centre bush tree
(1) Cut back a single-stemmed, one-year-old tree to about 1 m (3 ft).
(2) In the second year, cut back leaders by about two-thirds, keeping the centre open. (3) In the third year, cut back the leading shoots again by two-thirds and nip back laterals to about three buds. (4) In the fourth year, cut back the leaders by one-third and nip back laterals to three buds. The framework of an open-centre bush tree has now been formed.

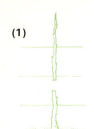

(1)

Pruning to form a fan
(1) Cut back one-year-old tree to about 60 cm (2 ft). **(2)** In the second summer, select two side shoots and train them along canes set at 45° on each side of the main stem. Remove all other shoots. In early spring cut back these laterals to about 60 cm (2 ft).

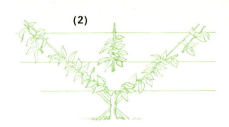

(2)

(3)

(3) In the third summer, train four shoots from each lateral against canes arranged in a fan shape. Rub out any buds that are pointing forwards or backwards. Allow buds pointing up or down to grow out and form sub-laterals. In early spring cut back main laterals to about 50 cm (20 in)

Pruning of free-standing plums and cherries should be limited to the cutting out of crossing branches and dead wood and the best time for this is May. Large pruning cuts should always be painted over immediately with a wound protector or bitumen paint.

Root pruning

Root pruning was at one time advocated as a means of controlling over-vigorous fruit trees. Severing of the tap-root was occasionally suggested prior to the cutting back of some of the other main roots. Care was necessary otherwise the root anchorage was insufficient to protect the tree against damage from gales.

The need to consider root pruning is no longer important or practical, it is far better to replace old, unprofitable trees with good varieties worked on modern rootstocks; rootstocks that do not need the attention of an axe or a saw during the lifetime of the tree.

Bark ringing

This was a technique which involved cutting out a track or tracks in the bark down to the hard wood of the tree. It was usual to suggest that the tracks should be 1 to 2.5 cm ($\frac{1}{2}$ to 1 in) wide according to the age of the tree, that they should not completely circle the trunk, three quarters the way round was customary with the breaks in the tracks on opposite sides of the trunk.

The theory was that bark ringing slowed down the flow of sap and consequently restricted the growth of the tree, thereby inducing fruit production. However, in practice, the cut bark quickly calloused over the tracks and the growth rate was then again back to normal with often the addition of a canker problem due to the wounds. The advent of dwarfing rootstocks has made bark ringing obsolete, and in any case it was never very effective.

Fertilisers

In fruit growing the trees or bushes usually stay put for a considerable number of years, taking out of the ground the same soluble nutrients year after year, so unless the essential elements for tree health and cropping are replaced regularly both health and cropping suffer. Although fertilisers are sometimes called 'artificial' because they are man made, all the elements they supply can be found in an average soil sample. However, when the ground is being continuously cropped they are seldom present in sufficient quantities for maximum crop yields of quality fruit. The essential elements are nitrogen (N), phosphorus (P) and potassium (K), these are available separately or combined together in what is called a balanced fertiliser such as Growmore. In the first instance the Growmore fertiliser formulation was designed for vegetable growing but it is just as suitable for supplying the three essential elements to most fruit crops.

With the ground well prepared at tree planting time nothing more than a small handful of bonemeal is needed to mix in with the filling-in soil. It is after establishment that the regular annual fertiliser application pays off. I apply Growmore to all our fruit crops at the end of February, at the rate of 60 to 90 g per sq m (2 to 3 ounces per sq yd). This early application allows time for the late winter rains to wash the fertiliser down to within reach of the roots.

As an alternative to Growmore fertiliser, which is 100% inorganic, I would recommend fish, blood and bone fertiliser which is organic based and somewhat slower acting but is released over a longer period.

The advantage of organic fertilisers is that they do at the same time supply minute but sufficient quantities of various trace elements. I well remember a deficiency problem on heavy clay at Thurgarton in Nottinghamshire, when, after making many attempts to solve a deficiency problem on raspberries, we switched our annual applications over to a meat and bone fertiliser with complete success.

Nitrogen provides the energy for growth, potash is the factor that increases fruit sweetness, colour and size and also plays a considerable role in the health of the tree or plant. There was a time when phosphates were said to be wasted on tree fruits but more recent work has shown that there is a relationship between a low level of phosphates and the incidence of mildew. Without a good potash level in the soil it is not possible to grow satisfactory crops of Cox's Orange Pippin apples; in fact, this is the most common cause for Cox having a reputation of being a difficult apple to grow.

When the level of potash becomes too high magnesium-deficiency symptoms may appear in the leaves, taking the form of yellowing between the veins. So successful fertiliser application is a question of striking a happy medium.

Foliar feeding
The application of nutrients in solution as an overhead spray is now an accepted method for obtaining a quick response; for instance when a tree or plant is showing signs of stress midway through a growing season and a traditional fertiliser application might take too long to relieve the situation a foliar feed would induce a much quicker response. I regard foliar feeding as a first-aid method for helping fruit trees or plants over a difficult period and certainly not as a complete substitute for the more orthodox nutrition systems which I prefer, namely the application of a balanced fertiliser at the end of February.

Having made that point, I am prepared to concede the fact that balanced fertilisers such as Growmore do not usually include in their formulations the trace elements. Most foliar-feed products are based on urea, a quick-acting source of nitrogen which is readily absorbed by the foliage and transported without much delay throughout the plant. In addition, the foliar-feed formulation will probably include some potash and phosphates and certainly a longish list of trace elements including iron and magnesium which are fairly common deficiencies. Fortunately iron and magnesium are capable of foliage absorption, so in cases when the foliage is inclined to be chlorotic it could be an iron deficiency, or when the yellowing is between the veins it might be a magnesium deficiency.

The most common cause of poor foliage colour is shortage of nitrogen, the leaves look starved and are a pale colour. It is in such cases that foliage feeding gives a quick almost spectacular response. In such cases the treatment could be repeated two or three weeks later with advantage.

Trace elements
In addition to the major elements nitrogen (N), phosphorus (phosphates, P_2O_5), potash (K_2O) and calcium, a number of minor elements need to be available in the soil otherwise the health and the cropping capacity of fruit are at risk. In most soils these so called trace elements are present and available in sufficient quantities to meet the needs of most plants without the interference of man. The deficiencies often occur when either the demands are too great due maybe to intensive monoculture or the locking-up of a particular trace element. This can result from an excessive amount of a major element being present in the soil. For instance, too much potash may be a contributing factor in a case of magnesium deficiency; too high a soil pH level may be the cause of manganese, boron or iron deficiencies. In other words excess available calcium can make manganese, boron and iron unavailable to plants. There are other additional complications such as the interdependence of both major and minor elements. For instance the uptake of calcium, phosphate and magnesium is inter-related, when one is missing or in short supply the other two are less effective.

Fortunately, due to the fact that liming is seldom recommended for fruit, cases of manganese, boron and iron deficiencies usually only occur on soil with a naturally high pH or those with calcareous subsoils. Magnesium deficiency, on the other hand, is fairly common and is due to regular applications of fertilisers with high levels of potash. The usual corrective treatment is commercial Epsom salts (magnesium sulphate) applied at the rate of 60 g per sq m (2 oz per sq yd). In addition to those mentioned, there are other essential trace elements but as they are present and freely available in practically all soils, there is no purpose in considering them here.

Those who wish to ensure that all the essential trace elements are in their fruit-growing soil can do so by applying a mixture of them in a special formulation in which they are released very slowly; this mixture should be applied during the winter.

Above: Dark healthy foliage
Below: Pale chlorotic foliage of plant suffering from magnesium deficiency
Opposite: Decorative and useful crab apples (see page 52)

Quality and Storage

Many factors affect the quality of fruit, some of which are in our power to influence, others, such as the climate of the district or the basic type of soil, we can do little about except to grow our fruit within the limitations imposed on us. The effect of climate and soil types has already been dealt with.

Fruit quality

The first step on the road to fruit quality is taken when a particular variety is selected for planting. It matters little what type of fruit it is unless the variety chosen has the essential good qualities to recommend it. Whilst this may not be so important in the case of soft fruits where mistakes made can easily be corrected fairly quickly with only a single season or two lost, fruit-tree-planting mistakes may only be discovered or the full consequences be realised after a lapse of several years, when it may be too late to start all over again.

For me the first essential quality in any fruit is flavour, without putting this at the top of the list it is difficult to justify fruit growing in the garden. The commercial fruit growers, certainly at the present time, do not head their list of priorities with flavour, if they did their yields and profits might fall to start with but would no doubt recover as the public rediscovered flavours they had given up as lost.

Yield, of course, must come next on our list, the capacity of a variety to crop in any particular district is important. Here again the performance of a variety may vary tremendously from district to district. Flavour is a basic quality in a variety of fruit, without it being there naturally no cultivation methods can put it there. However, when good flavour is

Opposite: easy-to-grow gooseberries (see page 57)

a natural quality already in the plant it can be improved and brought out to the full extent by nutritional expertise.

For instance, the application of sulphate of potash to the soil increases the sugar content and the flavour in most fruits; at the same time it enhances the fruit colour. Crop yields are related to the overall treatment of the soil within the limits of any particular variety. Strawberries and raspberries always do well if they start off with organically-based fertilisers such as blood, fish and bone.

Fruit trees do better when planted without the addition of soil enrichers such as compost or manure; the feeding for quality starts in the second February after planting when an application of a balanced fertiliser such as Growmore will result in tree health and fruit quality.

Freshness in home-grown fruit is a quality which cannot be purchased. To take full advantage of it the fruit should be picked when it is at its peak, not a day before or a day too late.

Fruit storage

Apples must be perfectly ripe at the time of picking if it is planned to store them. It is unwise to gather them before they leave the branch freely and if it is necessary to give the fruit a tug they are certainly not ready. Too early picking results in the fruit shrivelling and early rotting. To test for ripeness lift the fruit gently upwards and, if ready, the stalk will part from the branch without even a gentle pull.

Not all varieties of apple are suitable for storage, generally speaking it is the late-maturing ones that keep well for long periods. Pears should not be allowed to fully ripen on the tree as this results in gritty flesh instead of the more luscious juicy flesh enjoyed when the same variety is mature but still unripe at the time of picking. Most pears have a short storage life and need watching almost daily if losses through over-ripeness are to be avoided. Fruit intended for storage must be handled very carefully, bruising will lead to rotting and must be avoided. Any fruits

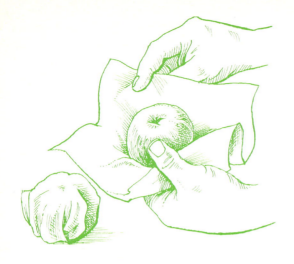

and stored in the freezer in the shortest possible time. The best varieties for freezing are those which have a good flavour; poor flavoured fruit will be even less tasty after freezing.

I think that raspberries, blackberries and the related berries such as loganberries, top the list of fruits for freezing. But cherries, strawberries and all the currants can be a great asset during the winter if used within their limitations.

The fruits belonging to the plum family are excellent for freezing, particularly damsons which retain their flavour best. The other soft tree fruits such as peaches and nectarines will retain their flavour but not their colour. Cooking apples freeze well but dessert apples are too soft as a rule. Pears are a disappointment as they discolour easily and tend to be very mushy when thawed.

Not many of us have a surplus of grapes and melons but if this happens they can be frozen too. I have seen and eaten grapes frozen as a bunch; they were delicious.

Another advantage of freezing fruit is that at the time of ripening we can be too busy to use the fruit for making jams and other preserves; fruit kept in the freezer can be used for this purpose at a future date when time is not at a premium.

damaged by pests and disease should never be stored but set aside for immediate use.

Fruit intended for storing should be dry at the time of picking and, if the weather is warm, allowed to cool before being put into store. Small quantities of fruit can be wrapped separately in soft paper, special oiled apple wraps are available for the purpose. Separation in this way prevents the risk of a mass outbreak of rotting; if a single fruit starts to rot the trouble is then confined and can soon be detected during a regular inspection.

Whilst length of storage time depends on the variety, the storage conditions are important – very dry, warm conditions should be avoided, especially centrally-heated rooms. A box with air holes for ventilation could be a substitute for a fruit room if it was kept in a cool airy place and regularly inspected.

Fruit for freezing

The advent of the freezer has solved practically all our glut problems, many more fruits can be frozen than can be preserved by bottling. Some fruits are obviously more suitable for freezing than others and the soft fruits top the list of suitability, although most tree fruits can also be successfully kept in the freezer. In all cases the fruit must be ripe but not overripe and the soft fruits particularly must be dry when gathered and then prepared

Pest Control

Without exception all our fruit crops can at some time or other suffer from pest or disease damage. Unless controlled, some of these pests and diseases are capable of completely ruining a crop and worse still may undermine the health of the plant.

Pest control

Pests can be divided into two groups, those that suck the sap from the foliage or fruit and those that chew their way into fruit or foliage. To control the sucking insects a contact insecticide can be used which kills when the chemical is absorbed through their bodies. An alternative is to apply a systemic insecticide which may be effective in two ways: by direct body absorption or by translocation within the plant foliage where it stays put and will remain effective for a period of time to await the arrival of the sucking insect for its first feed on the lethal sap.

Chewing pests, such as caterpillars, are controlled by spraying their intended food with what we call a stomach poison. Fortunately as a result of much research, insecticides are now available which, although effective against the insects, are safe to use and are not harmful to man or domestic animals, provided of course that the directions on the packs are read and strictly followed.

The repeated use of an insecticide based on a single active ingredient should be avoided, it is wise to ring the changes, otherwise a race of resistant insects may build up.

For efficient pest control the timing is often most important. Practically every insect has a vulnerable stage in its life and it is at these times that the insecticide does its job most effectively, whereas spraying too late or too early may be a waste of time.

Generally speaking, spraying with liquid formulations is more effective than dust-based insecticides of the same active ingredients. The insecticides I use on my fruit are:

Contact insecticides: malathion, HCH (BHC), fentrothion and derris
Systemic insecticides: dimethoate
Stomach poisons: HCH (BHC), fentrothion and derris
Acaricide: dinocap

Derris is of vegetable origin and is safe but less effective than the newer organic compounds. Fentrothion has replaced DDT for caterpillar control without associated long-term problems, fruit may be harvested 14 days after spraying. Malathion is one of the safest insecticides, sprayed fruit may be harvested 24 hours later. Fruit sprayed with dimethoate can be harvested after one week. HCH- (BCH-) sprayed fruit can be harvested after 2 weeks. Dinocap can be added to sprays for red spider mite control. Lime sulphur is used against big bud mite on blackcurrants, but some varieties are sulphur sensitive (see p.54).

Detailed instructions regarding the particular pests and the timing of the applications are supplied with the products. Do make sure to read the directions carefully before spraying.

Wasps

The wasp problem varies from year to year; it is seldom related to the number of queen wasps around in the late spring or early summer. Climatic factors between then and fruit-ripening time must play a large role in

Hang a jam jar half filled with beer on plum trees to lure wasps away from fruit

Spray Programme for Apples and Pears

Time of application	Chemical	Pest or Disease
November to February	Tar oil wash	eggs of overwintering insects
bud burst	captan malathion or a systemic insecticide dinocap	scab sucking insects red spider mite
green bud	captan malathion or a systemic insecticide dinocap	scab sucking insects red spider mite
pink or white bud	captan malathion or a systemic insecticide dinocap fenitrothion	scab sucking insects red spider mite codling moth
petal fall	captan malathion or a systemic insecticide dinocap fenitrothion	scab sucking insects red spider mite codling moth
fruitlet	captan malathion or a systemic insecticide dinocap fenitrothion	scab sucking insects red spider mite codling moth

determining how many nests build up to full activity. Plum-ripening time usually coincides with wasp activity. Destruction of the nests is obviously the best way of dealing with the problem. A wasp-destroyer product inserted into the entrance of the nest which is then sealed off immediately is the most effective answer but this must be done at dusk when all the wasps are at home. In cases where the nests cannot be located or are inaccessible, jam jars half filled with thin syrup or beer hung on the trees should prove more attractive than the plums. Beer is probably the best bait; the wasps being happily drunk when they fall backwards to drown in the liquid. The jars should be checked frequently, emptied and the bait replaced, otherwise the mass of dead wasps will simply provide a landing place for the living to drink in safety before returning to feed on the plums.

Bird damage control

Insect pests on fruit are fairly easy to control, modern insecticides are effective when applied at the right time and few people bemoan the elimination of either greenfly or caterpillars. However it is an entirely different situation when the pests are feathered. In this country it is common practice to feed the birds and many gardeners go to the length of setting up feeding places. Specially designed bird tables are often erected with separate feeding contraptions to provide for the needs of the seed eaters as well as the others which may prefer scraps of meat, bread or other left-over food. Birds feeding on a table near a window can give great pleasure, but birds, like many other creatures, quickly develop habits. Where the birds find food freely available in the winter, a time when the going is tough elsewhere, is obviously a desirable place of residence for the rest of the year too. The lesson to be learned here is that the more you feed the birds the greater your local bird population; population densities are always determined by the availability of food.

Blackbirds especially are nature's distributors of fruit seeds, from the beginning of time the wild fruits were produced in attractive colours and when ripe filled with sweetness.

The blackbirds did a service by eating the fruit and scattering the seed in their excreta far and wide over the countryside, so it is not surprising that they should still wish to carry on with their role in nature's overall plan.

Other birds such as the bullfinch have changed their feeding habits, maybe of necessity so as to survive in our quickly changing environment. Now with the bullfinch population so widely distributed and on the increase, its preference for a diet based on fruit buds rather than weed seeds has brought this most beautiful bird into disgrace, in fact, its activities from Christmas until bud burst has made it the fruit growers' enemy number one. A single pair of bullfinches can systematically denude every fruit tree of any buds within their reach, leaving only the odd fruit bud at the extreme tips of the thin branches.

Our first approach to the problem was an attempt to make the fruit buds distasteful. We found that this could be done by spraying the trees with a dilute suspension of bird deterrent chemicals. The results were satisfactory when the weather remained dry but unfortunately it has not been possible to formulate the chemicals so that the spray deposits are weather resistant. Repeated applications after rain are essential and even so, bullfinch damage can occur before the weather improves sufficiently to permit re-spraying.

At my farm the problem became so serious that complete netting in of apples, pears, plums and cherries was considered as a practical possibility. Fortunately most of our apples are on a dwarfing rootstock such as Malling 9, so it was not too difficult to keep the trees down to below a 2 m (6 ft) maximum but our pears on Quince C rootstock needed to lose at least 1 m (3 ft) of their height. The trained plums and cherries on a fence presented no such problems, so an overall 2 m-(6 ft-) high fruit cage was erected and proved in the first season to be the complete answer to the bullfinch menace.

After trying out fruit cages with less height for soft fruit, we settled for 2 m (6 ft) again as being more practical for raspberries and other cane fruits, with strawberries interplanted as

Erecting a fruit cage is the complete answer to preventing bird damage

required. We now grow all our soft fruit without sharing the crops with the blackbirds. However, it is important to peg the netting down well otherwise they walk in and feast. Heavy snowfalls can present problems but removal of the top netting will reduce the likelihood of collapse. Galvanised wire netting with a 2·5 cm (1 in) mesh is obviously stronger than plastic netting but its use as a covering for crops such as raspberries usually results in a zinc toxicity problem after one or two seasons. The introduction of a fruit cage is a worthwhile investment which provides the means to combat the problem without harming the birds or upsetting our bird-loving neighbours.

I have tried many other methods including long strips of aluminium foil which sparkle and move in the wind, and expensive coloured bird scarers, only to find that the birds soon accept them as part of the environment – it is not uncommon to find nests of young birds in a scarecrow. Nylon web does work but the difficulty of completely removing the fibre from the fruit is a great problem.

Disease control

Most fruit diseases result from either fungal or bacterial infections which when established are difficult or impossible to eradicate. The wise fruit grower aims at prevention rather than cure because in most instances by the time the symptoms of the disease appear the damage to the fruit or foliage has already been done and it is already too late to take any effective action.

Impoverished trees and plants are more prone to disease than those receiving balanced feeding, so the first step after purchasing healthy stock is to ensure that none of the essential major or minor nutritional elements are lacking during the growing season. Routine management such as pruning in the right way and at the right time is also important; overcrowded branches create a micro-climate within the tree conducive to disease problems and make control spraying less effective. Removal of diseased fruit, foliage or wood is comparable to weeding before the weeds seed and it gradually reduces the problem. Painting of large cut surfaces with bitumen prevents fungi or bacteria entering the wood.

The most common disease of apples and pears is scab which is responsible for the ill-shapen fruits with rough black patches. The fungus spores are released during warm, damp weather. I start spraying with captan at the bud burst stage and carry on with repeats at green bud, pink or white bud and again at petal fall followed by a fruitlet stage application. The pre-blossom applications are the most important, an uncontrolled infection at that stage produces the largest scab lesions, whereas from the fruitlet stage onwards an infection only produces small patches or even tiny spots.

Canker can affect both apples and pears. It is caused by a fungus which gains entry into the bark, usually through a wound. Any break in the bark caused either by man, insect or nature can afford it entry. Unless dealt with quickly, canker eats into the wood causing in extreme cases the loss of large branches. Action taken in the early stages is effective; scrape all the roughened bark away down to completely clean wood and paint the wound area with either a wound or bitumen paint. Canker is often a greater problem on poorly-drained or very heavy soils.

Apple mildew is reduced by pruning and the immediate removal of the silvery fruit buds in the spring. All prunings and diseased material should be destroyed as soon as possible. The addition of dinocap to the captan spray mix will keep the current season's foliage clean and limit the re-appearance of the fungus the following season.

With diseases such as brown rot of apples it is a question of removing and destroying the infected fruit.

Botrytis (grey mould) and mildew on strawberries can be minimised by routine removal of dead foliage and attacked fruit. Systemic fungicides such as benomyl, applied early enough at the pre- and post-blossom stages can be very effective. Benomyl is also valuable on gooseberries, blackcurrants and raspberries when applied as a routine preventive treatment against mildew.

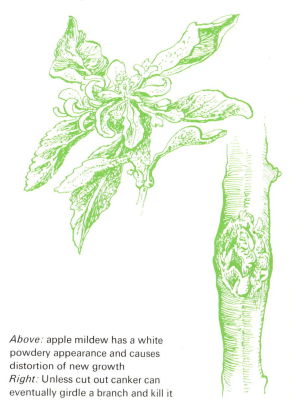

Above: apple mildew has a white powdery appearance and causes distortion of new growth
Right: Unless cut out canker can eventually girdle a branch and kill it

Virus diseases

Unlike some fungal diseases a virus disease cannot be treated with any prospect of success once it is established within a plant. In most cases the health of the plant deteriorates with increasing rapidity until its productive

35

capacity is completely destroyed and death ultimately occurs.

Virus diseases are very infectious and those attacking fruit are no exceptions, in most cases the virus is carried from plant to plant by sucking insects or by such media as tools used for pruning. All that is needed for the transmission of a virus disease from an infected plant to a healthy specimen is a minute trace of the virus-carrying sap. Sucking insects such as aphids are usually the culprits moving as they do from plant to plant, inserting their mouth-parts (proboscis) into the foliage as they go in search of food.

Soft fruits are subject to virus diseases especially raspberries, strawberries and black-currants and it is impossible to stress too strongly the importance of purchasing certified virus-free stock and the need to control sucking insects by routine spraying.

It is folly to propagate from fruiting plants unless the health status of the parent plants is absolutely beyond suspicion; acceptance of gift plants can prove very expensive.

The symptoms of raspberry mosaic virus appear in the leaves as mottling with both light- and dark-green areas, in severe cases the leaves curl and become deformed with yellowish spots or patches in them. In cases of this kind leaf size decreases, as does the growth of the young canes, and slowly but surely the fruiting deteriorates to almost zero. It is wise to burn infected canes before re-planting with new healthy stock. Some varieties, such as Norfolk Giant, can be carriers without succumbing to the virus disease, whilst others such as Lloyd George are able to offer little resistance.

Two virus diseases in particular attack strawberries, one is yellow edge, so named because the young leaves develop yellowish margins; infected plants become dwarf and unfruitful. The other important virus disease is crinkle which in its severe form causes the leaves to crinkle up; again the plants are soon dwarfed and quickly become unprofitable.

Eradication by lifting and burning the infected plants is essential. Replanting with healthy plants can follow. Routine aphid

control is the only safeguard against a repeat of the trouble. Unfortunately the best-flavoured strawberry, Royal Sovereign, is most susceptible to both virus diseases.

Reversion in blackcurrants with loss of cropping is due to a virus carried by the big

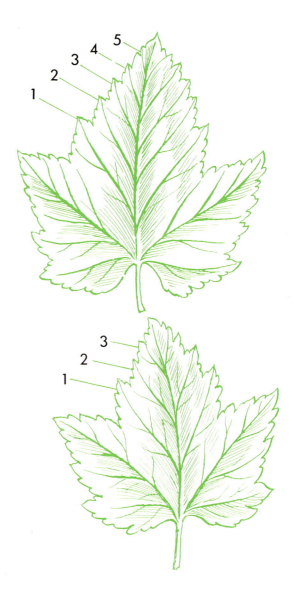

Reversion disease of blackcurrant is apparent in the foliage.
Top: A healthy leaf has five main veins in the central lobe and a deep cleft between the basal lobes.
Bottom: A leaf affected with reversion has only three main veins in the central lobe and the cleft is much less pronounced

bud mite. Reverted bushes have small nettle-shaped leaves rather than the large 6 to 8 pointed leaves found on a healthy bush. Again eradication by lifting and burning must be recommended together with big bug mite control spraying with sulphur in the future.

A Ministry of Agriculture's certificate of health is evidence that the nursery stock was inspected during the growing season and found to be healthy, I would suggest that such a certificate is essential when buying soft fruit plants or canes. The scheme has recently been extended to cover apples, pears, plums and cherries. There are two levels of certificates; A (ordinary) which requires the varieties to be true to name, vigorous, healthy and appreciably free from pests and diseases and SS (special stock), or EMLA as it is often called, which indicates that the propagation was from virus-free parent stock. Unfortunately this super-level stock is still in short supply but supplies will improve as more nurseries operate under the strict controls demanded for this higher certificate.

Spraying equipment
There are few fruits that are not troubled at some time or other during the growing season by pests and/or diseases. Fortunately most of these are controllable if the right treatments are applied at the right time in an efficient manner.

A good sprayer of a suitable size is essential, the type and size of the equipment should be related to the area of fruit and the size of the trees or bushes to be sprayed. For strawberries a small hand sprayer may suffice but for cane and bush fruit a larger one with more capacity and higher pressure may be needed, whilst for tree fruits an even larger and more powerful piece of equipment would be required. Whatever is used the insecticides or fungicides applied will only be as effective as the sprayer and the person using it allows them to be. Good coverage of the foliage, and in some cases the young fruitlets, is essential if the anti-pest or disease applications are to be successful.

Compressed air sprayers, which are pumped up prior to spraying, are now preferred to the old knapsack-type sprayer which needed pumping continuously throughout the operation. Size of nozzle aperture pre-determines the type of spray pattern, a coarse or fine mist spray can be obtained at will with the same sprayer by simply changing the nozzle. Nozzles with large holes give a coarser spray than those with smaller holes. A coarse spray pattern would be required for winter spraying whereas a much finer spray pattern would be efficient when the sprayer was used for the application of either systemic insecticides or fungicides.

The use of sprayers with a capacity of 4·5 to 9 litres (1 to 2 gal) can be effort consuming, as can the pumping up exercise. For those who wish for an easier yet still efficient approach to pest and disease control, I would consider the merits of a smaller sprayer with a capacity of 3·4 litres ($\frac{3}{4}$ gal) which is powered by a re-chargeable battery. It is ideal for senior citizens who still wish to grow clean fruit without the risk to their health.

A compressed air sprayer

Apples

Apples are the most important of our hardy tree fruits, our temperate climate is one of the best in the world for quality apples and we can benefit from this fact by choosing the varieties which are well suited to our own district. Apples can be successfully grown on most types of soil found in the United Kingdom below an altitude of 180 m (600 ft); on sites at a higher level growing problems creep in.

Choosing a site

Good soil drainage is essential as short periods of waterlogging can cause root death. Heavy soils with poor general drainage fail to give the trees a chance; growth is unhealthy and canker develops on the more susceptible apple varieties. Drainage in the top 1·25 m (4 ft) must always be good. For trees on a vigorous rootstock the good drainage depth needs to be greater as the roots, once the tree is established, will be drawing nutrients and moisture from up to a depth of 3 m (10 ft) or even more.

When the drainage is satisfactory it is usually possible to deal with other matters such as control of fertility levels. Some soils have a naturally high fertility whilst others are poor and need more attention. However, the use of fertilisers can make the necessary corrections for the achievement of good cropping results.

Soils of low fertility are often thin sandy types lacking the ability to hold moisture, on these artificial watering may be needed from time to time during the growing season. Apples do best on soils with pH levels slightly below 7, in other words they are happier on slightly acid soils and for this reason chalky soils are not very suitable. Soils with high pH sub-soils can also present problems for when the roots reach a calcareous stratum the foliage may become chlorotic, a condition which can sometimes be corrected by spraying with chelated iron or manganese (chemicals which are specially prepared and sold for this purpose).

The secret of growing apples successfully in our own garden is to appreciate the limitations imposed by the site, prepare for the planting accordingly, opt for the most suitable rootstocks and choose only varieties known to do well in the district.

Very rich soils such as those found in the average vegetable garden will probably have too high a nitrogen level for dessert apples and my advice is against mixing vegetable and apple growing – it is far better to have a separate site.

Another factor that goes against the production of quality dessert apples is high rainfall, an ideal yearly average rainfall would be 60 cm (24 in); above 100 cm (40 in) culinary varieties do much better and are a sounder proposition. If the site is exposed, some form of shelter against wind may be needed but it would be a mistake to plant apples very close to other trees or buildings, as they will need as much sunshine as possible and no competition from already established trees. Protection against wind becomes more difficult near the coast where there is the added problem of sea air; apples do not enjoy sea air and seldom do well within the sound of the waves.

Wherever possible plant on the higher ground. This is a precaution against the risk of a spring-frost-damage problem since cold air like water flows downhill, so if you can let it get away so much the better; I have known a case where just opening the gate at the lower end of the orchard did the trick.

Rootstocks

The particular rootstock to be ordered is most important, all apple varieties are now either budded or grafted on special rootstocks. The complete list of rootstocks would be lengthy but for the garden fruit grower a short practical list would include the following:

Malling 9, a dwarfing rootstock for cordons for planting on really good soils.

Malling 26 is a slightly less dwarfing rootstock for cordons, dwarf pyramids and bush trees.

MM 106, a semi-dwarfing rootstock for bush and espalier-trained trees.

MM 111, a more vigorous rootstock for half-standard trees.

Planting

A glance at the list will reveal the dangers of planting apples without knowledge of the rootstock, no aftercare can alter the basic growth factors of the rootstock which will always determine or try to determine the size of the tree, in spite of anything you do. Cordons on Malling 9 take up least space, I plant them 1 m (3 ft) apart with the stems sloping away from the sun at an angle of 45 degrees. Dwarf pyramid trees staked and tied can be planted 1·25 m (4 ft) apart with 1·25 m (4 ft) between the rows. Bush trees on Malling 26 rootstock, staked and tied, can be planted at 3 m (10 ft) apart but if the trees are on MM 106 rootstock I would plant no closer than 4 m (13 ft) and, thinking of the ultimate tree size, would prefer to place then 5·5 m (18 ft) apart. Half-standard trees on MM 111 rootstock should be staked and tied at 7·5 m (24 ft) apart with even more space between vigorous varieties. Espalier-trained trees on MM 106 rootstock on walls and fences should not be planted closer than 4 m (13 ft) apart and a few extra feet would be an advantage.

With the rootstock question settled, how old should the young tree to be planted be? I have no hesitation in always planting and recommending the planting of maiden trees (one year old); older trees take so much longer to establish and nothing is gained timewise in buying the more expensive two- or three-year-old trees.

Pests and diseases

Codling moth is the pest responsible for many of the maggots inside apples, the apples which fall and ripen earlier than the rest. Egg laying occurs during the period of June and July, but in exceptional seasons may be extended until September. The eggs are laid on the leaves or fruits and 10 to 14 days later the caterpillars emerge and start to feed and work their way through the skin of the fruit towards the core. Control measures consist of spraying with stomach poison insecticides such as derris, fenitrothion or liquid HCH (BHC). A band of corrugated paper tied around the tree trunks early in July will trap a number of the caterpillars on their way down to pupate. Inspect these traps about fruit-picking time.

For other pests and diseases see chapter on Pest Control, page 31.

Codling moth is a serious pest of apples
Left: Corrugated paper tied around the trunk will trap caterpillars on their way to pupate. Change the paper regularly.
Below: An apple infested with codling moth

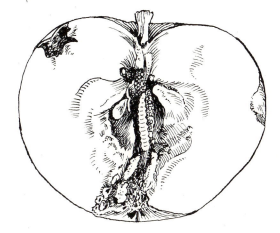

Varieties

Finally comes the question of varieties, here the list of possibilities is lengthy even if the planting is to be done in one of the less favoured climatic areas.

Up in the cooler parts I would make a selection from the following:

Dessert – Charles Ross, Discovery, Egremont Russet, Epicure, Fortune, James Grieve, Lord Lambourne, Red Ellison and Worcester Pearmain.

Culinary – Arthur Turner, Grenadier, Lord Derby, Rev. W. Wilks

For a garden in a known frost pocket I would certainly consider:

Dessert – Discovery, Epicure, Golden Delicious, James Grieve, Red Ellison, Worcester Pearmain

Culinary – Lord Derby

Not all gardeners are prepared to carry out each year a complete pest and disease control programme plus routine pruning, fortunately there are a few varieties which grow tidily and need the minimum of spray treatments, so for those who want to grow apples the easy way I would recommend:

Dessert – Charles Ross, Discovery, Egremont Russet, Epicure, Fortune, Red Ellison and Sunset.

Culinary – Grenadier, Rev. W. Wilks and Newton Wonder.

CULINARY VARIETIES

Arthur Turner: this is a large round conical-shaped cooking apple which is often planted for its wonderful show of blossom rather than its fruit, which is not equal in cooking qualities to those in the list that follows. The skin is greenish-yellow with a brownish-red flush, the flesh is white. It is a vigorous upright grower, a regular and heavy cropper, in fact an ornamental tree with a bonus. Season August/October. Mid-season flowering.

Bramley's Seedling: our finest late-keeping apple, unfortunately it is not one of the easiest to grow. Unless planted on a dwarfing root-stock it makes a very large tree; it is very susceptible to spring-frost damage and apple scab. Being a triploid, and therefore a bad pollinator, it really needs two good pollinators which should be planted nearby, I have used Discovery and Early Victoria. In a small garden I would plant Bramley on either a Malling 9 or Malling 26 rootstock and grow it as a small bush tree making sure that it was always well staked and tied. It is a large apple which holds well on the tree and should not be picked until the end of October for storing. Season November/March. Mid-season flowering.

Early Victoria (Emneth Early): one of the earliest cooking apples; the thinnings are good for stewing from the middle of July. It is medium sized, conical with yellowish-green skin, liable to be small unless well thinned in its 'on year' (it is a biennial cropper). The soft flesh is greenish-white and really delicious when cooked. A variety well suited to the small garden, being of moderate vigour with an upright and tidy growth habit. Season July/August. Mid-season flowering.

Grenadier: a larger apple than Early Victoria, which is ready about a month later. Subject to irregularities in shape but most fruits are round and conical. The skin is greenish-yellow and the white flesh is frothy when cooked. It is a regular cropper of moderate vigour and it would need to be on a dwarfing rootstock in a small garden. Season August/September. Mid-season flowering.

Howgate Wonder: a large keeping apple and regular and heavy cropper. At one time it was acclaimed to be the alternative to Bramley as a garden variety but its cooking qualities do not compare although it may be better looking. The skin is yellowish-green, slightly flushed with a few red stripes, it is frothy when cooked but lacks flavour. Makes a spreading, rather vigorous tree. Season November/February. Mid-season flowering.

Lane's Prince Albert: a large roundish apple which keeps till March, the skin is greenish-yellow with red streaks, the greenish-white flesh is soft and cooks well with good flavour. The tree has a spreading habit, with us it has been a regular cropper. At one time it was unpopular on account of its sensitivity to lime sulphur but that is now a fungicide of the past. It is a reliable variety and a sound alternative to Bramley. I can recommend it. Season November/March. Late flowering.

Lord Derby: a large oblong conical-shaped apple with an all too short keeping season. The skin is greenish-yellow, the white flesh is firm and somewhat acid; as a boy I enjoyed it straight off the tree. It cooks well and has flavour and often sets its fruit without pips. It is a vigorous grower and makes an upright tree, always a regular cropper wherever it is planted. Season October/November. Late flowering.

Newton Wonder: this is a large round apple with a characteristic short, thick, fleshy stalk. Whilst it is generally regarded as a cooking variety it is also of fair dessert quality when fully ripe. The skin is yellow with a red flush and streaks, the flesh is yellow and crisp, too acid for me now but I did enjoy it at one time straight off the tree. Its growth is vigorous, spreading in habit; it is a reasonable cropper in its 'on year' (it is a biennial cropper). Season November/March. Late flowering.

Rev. W. Wilks: a very large mid-season cooking apple of great quality, in my opinion it is our finest apple for baking or cooking during its all too short season. The skin is creamy white with slight flushing, the flesh is white and soft, which when cooked becomes frothy and has a wonderful flavour. We grow it as small bush trees on a Malling 9 rootstock, its growth habit is ideal for a small garden. It is a very heavy cropper in its 'on year' when it needs thinning to get the really large apples for baking. Season September/October. Early flowering.

DESSERT VARIETIES

Baker's Delicious: a quality apple which deserves to be more widely planted. Its regular cropping ability in most districts makes it a variety worth considering for planting in the northern areas of the country. The fruit is medium sized, rather variable in shape but mainly round-conical with pale-yellow skin flushed with orange-scarlet. The flesh is firm with an aromatic flavour. Season August/early September. Early flowering.

Blenheim Orange: an old variety with boyhood memories but now its large flattish apples turning yellow with a dullish-red flush never seem to me to have that full flavour I remember when each October I used to climb the large trees at home. Maybe it is a variety that will never be so good again. I regret not having returned to Cambridgeshire for a few grafts, then I would have been more sure of the variety. The real Blenheim Orange is a grand apple with a nutty flavour, its flesh is yellow and crisp and it is also a very good culinary apple. It is self-sterile and needs two pollinators which blossom at the same time. Season November/January. Mid-season flowering.

Charles Ross: this is one of the most reliable croppers, and as the fruit is always inclined to be large, thinning is seldom necessary. It is a very attractive apple, round, pale yellow with red stripes in its flushed cheeks. When fully ripe it is sweet and the flesh tender but it tends to go woolly after a few weeks. It is more susceptible to brown rot than most varieties. It is a variety to plant on chalky soils when a dual purpose apple is wanted. I grow it as a small bush tree on Malling 9 rootstock but for the majority of soils I would recommend MM 106 rootstock. Season October/December. Mid season flowering.

Cox's Orange Pippin: this is the dessert apple *par excellence* when well grown. Size of fruit varies considerably, it is generally larger when grown on dwarfing rootstocks. Its superb

Scab on Cox. Cracking and scab-like lesions disfigure the fruit

aromatic flavour is well known. Not suitable for planting in the colder districts or elsewhere in gardens unless it can be well looked after. Cox is particularly susceptible to apple scab and mildew. On poorly drained soils canker often becomes a problem. For healthy tree growth and good size of fruit potash is an essential nutrient. The fruit should not be picked too early, late October or early November is the time in our district. Season November/January. Mid-season flowering.

Crispin: an apple of the Golden Delicious type which came to this country from Japan originally under the name of Mutsu. I first grew it in Nottinghamshire where, contrary to expectation, it did well. The fruits are larger than Golden Delicious but with less flavour. It is a particularly good keeper, but its somewhat muddy skin complexion may have prevented it from becoming more popular. It is very vigorous and not in my opinion suitable for either growing as a cordon or a small bush tree but can be grown on an MM 106 rootstock. Season December/March. Mid-season flowering.

Discovery: a fairly recent introduction now well established as one of our best early dessert apples. Reputed to be a Worcester Pearmain

seedling, the fruit is round and flattish, medium size with the most attractive yellow to red colourings, fully ripe it is gorgeous even to look at in the fruit bowl. The firm flesh is full of flavour which reminds one of Cox and it never disappoints. Unlike most early apples it keeps for several weeks. It usually needs a couple of years to settle down before cropping well, from then on net the trees as the birds also prefer Discovery. It is a tip bearer (bears fruit on branch tips rather than laterals) like its parent. Season Mid-August/September. Mid-season flowering.

Egremont Russet: for those who like a russet apple here is one with excellent flavour, the fruit is medium sized, the flesh is yellow, juicy and firm. Well suited for the small garden as it is an upright grower. It is a reliable cropper but inclined to suffer from cracking unless well supplied with nutrients. In my experience very sensitive to boron deficiency which, until remedied did cause excessive russetting and cracking. Season October/December. Early flowering.

Epicure: originally known as Laxton's Epicure, a medium-sized flattish round apple, greenish yellow flushed with red. On its day when fully ripe it is truly delicious, so sweet and full of juice; the aromatic flavour appeals to me. Unfortunately the tender flesh does not keep well. The crop usually needs some thinning otherwise the fruit is inclined to be small. Season September. Mid-season flowering.

Fortune: is another Laxton variety with a unique aromatic flavour, medium size fruit, attractive yellow with red streaks. A really good apple in districts that suit it. Season September/October. Mid-season flowering.

Golden Delicious: this well-known apple is grown in great quantities on the continent. In this country the skin is never a clear yellow but always inclined to be a little muddy by comparison. When home grown and ripened on the tree the flavour and flesh quality can be excellent. In the southern half of the country it is a regular cropper, growth habit suits the small garden. Not an apple for northern districts. Season December/February. Late flowering.

Idared: this is a recent introduction with many good qualities, it is a very free cropper of medium-sized fruit with a good reddish colour. When ripe its flavour and sweetness make it more than acceptable as a dessert keeping apple. At all times it is a useful culinary apple. My one complaint against it is its susceptibility to apple mildew, routine control spraying is essential. Season November/April. Early flowering.

James Grieve: is probably the most popular garden apple, it is a regular cropper almost everywhere. It is a vigorous grower but behaves well on dwarfing rootstocks. The oval fruits are medium sized except on very young trees. Skin colour varies from a yellowish green to a yellowish red, depending on the nutritional status of the soil. The flesh is soft and bruises easily. Picked ripe from the tree it is delicious but the quality deteriorates quickly afterwards. Somewhat subject to brown rot and premature fruit drop. Season September/early October. Mid-season flowering.

Lord Lambourne: an excellent quality apple of medium size, round but often slightly flattish in shape. Seldom very brightly coloured, greenish yellow with crimson flush and streaks. The flesh is firm and crisp; when ripe the flavour is good and well suited to my own palate. When virus free its growth habit and capacity for regular cropping makes it an ideal tree for the small garden. Season October/November. Early flowering.

Red Ellison: this is a sport from the well known Ellison's Orange, when grown well with a reasonable level of potash in the fertiliser treatment, the skin colour is a beautiful bright red. Just as good as its parent in every respect including spring frost resistance. It has rather soft flesh when ripe, the flavour is aromatic with a touch of aniseed in it, not everyone's taste but I have always liked the Ellison's Orange flavour. It tends to make a lot of thin upright growth and to be a biennial cropper, nevertheless a useful garden variety. Season September/October. Late flowering.

Sunset: is a variety which is well worth considering in districts where Cox's Orange Pippin is a non-starter. It is a good alternative although not equal in quality to Cox but if thinned early and well the size of its flattish fruit is comparable. The flesh is firm with very good flavour somewhat resembling that of a Cox. Skin colour, golden yellow with a reddish flush and russet specks, is dull in comparison with Cox. Its compact growth and ability to crop regularly in the cooler areas has made it popular. Season November/December. Mid-season flowering.

Superb: known originally as Laxton's Superb, considered at one time as a possible alternative to Cox but it is a biennial bearer (crops heavily every other year). I have several times tried to break this habit but never with complete success. Its vigorous whippy growth has also reduced its popularity as a garden apple. Maybe I am prejudiced but I have never regarded it as a quality apple. Season November/February. Mid-season flowering.

Worcester Pearmain: the well-known early apple whose reputation has been spoiled by too early marketing. Grown at home and picked fully ripe from the tree it is full of juice, sweetness and flavour. Unfortunately when picked immature it is almost flavourless but picked ripe the flesh tends to go woolly and lose its flavour. It is now superseded by Discovery, another tip bearer but a far superior apple for late August. Season August/September. Late flowering.

Pollination Table for Apples

Early flowering	Mid-season flowering	Late flowering
Baker's Delicious	Arthur Turner	Allington Pippin
Beauty of Bath	Blenheim Orange	Cox's Pomona
Bismark	Bramley's Seedling (T)	Crawley Beauty
Egremont Russet	Charles Ross	Edward VII
Golden Spire	Cox's Orange Pippin	Ellison's Orange
Irish Peach	Crispin (T)	Gascoyne's Scarlet (T)
Keswick Codlin	Devonshire Quarrendon	Golden Delicious
Lord Lambourne	Discovery	Heusgen's Golden Reinette
Norfolk Beauty	Early Victoria	Lady Sudeley
Rev. W. Wilkes	Epicure	Lane's Prince Albert
Ribston Pippen	Exquisite	Lord Derby
Warner's King (T)	Fortune	Monarch
	Golden Noble	Newton Wonder
	Grenadier	Northern Greening
	Howgate Wonder	Orleans Reinette
	James Grieve	Red Ellison
	John Standish	Winston
	King of the Pippins	Worcester Pearmain
	King's Acre Pippin	
	Laxton's Superb	
	Merton Prolific	
	Merton Worcester	
	Peasgood's Nonsuch	
	Rival	
	Stirling Castle	
	Sturmer Pippin	
	Sunset	
	Tydeman's Early	
	Tydeman's Orange	

T – triploid, needs two pollinators

Opposite: Grow damsons for jam making (see page 55)

Apricots

I have come to the conclusion that the apricot, the earliest fruit tree to blossom in the UK, can only be cropped outdoors in the more favoured districts such as the south-west. On my farm we have two very healthy fan-trained trees on a west-facing fence. The training and pruning has been precisely carried out and we have had plenty of spur blossom each February but, alas, try as we may some time between February and May a frost comes along to destroy either the blossom or the small fruitlets.

Protection

During the autumn of 1977 we covered the trees with plastic sheeting, at the same time making provision for ventilation, as high temperatures can be just as deadly as frosts; unfortunately the plastic sheeting was of no avail, a frost with the temperature down to −6°C (21°F) in mid-April left us without a single apricot fruitlet.

Fish netting or old curtain material provides better protection against frost than plastic film.

Given the protection of a greenhouse apricots are still more difficult than peaches, as temperatures above 7°C (45°F) before the fruitlets stone leads to trouble and even after the fruitlets have got past that critical stage higher temperatures in the range of 13° to 16°C (55°F to 60°F) may cause fruit drop.

Planting

I mention our sad experiences as I would not wish to mislead, so what follows is for the favoured few in the south-west who may have a south-facing wall about 4 m (13 ft) high. Apricots are not too fussy about soil type but it must be well drained, if it is calcareous so much the better, the lime in the soil will be an aid to stoning, always a critical stage in the swelling of the young fruitlets.

I would always recommend late October or early November for the planting of young two-year-old fan-trained trees. It is best to plant the trees with their stems at the base a few inches in front of the wall. The addition of bonemeal and filling in with fine soil helps root establishment and growth. As with all trees planted against a wall, drying out of the soil must be guarded against; watering may often be necessary and certainly will be early in the new year. Varieties of apricots are limited, pollination is not a problem as all are self-fertile.

Protect apricot trees from frost early in the year by covering the branches with netting

Opposite: A well-trained grape vine (see page 59)

Pruning

Pruning should be limited to disbudding, pinching out the young unwanted shoots and stopping the growth of the branches as necessary, and all this is done as early as possible during the growing season with the minimum of pruning left for the winter. The unwanted young growths are those that either grow downwards, inwards or outwards, the shoots breaking from the upper sides of the branches are the ones to take care of for tying in as soon as practical, in this way the expanding fan shape is retained.

Varieties

The varieties we have tried are Farmingdale and Alfred but we have been unsuccessful in cropping these.

Blackberries

The wild blackberries found in our less cared for hedgerows have the best flavour but even these vary considerably in size of berry and flavour. So if the decision is made to plant a wild blackberry the selection should be carefully made.

Care and cultivation

Look for a bush with large fruits at picking time, one usually finds a cane or two on the bush which has rooted at the tip. Cut it below the roots and pot this up into a 13 cm (5 in) pot and keep it growing till November, the best planting out time. A wild blackberry plant without hedgerow competition becomes even stronger growing and needs just as much training attention as the cultivated varieties.

Like all cane fruits blackberries do best in a well-drained soil, they do not object to partial shade and, in fact, enjoy it if the ground does not dry out during the growing season. Mulching with well-rotted compost or manure improves cropping especially on poor soils, as does an application of Growmore fertiliser in March.

Tip layering of a blackberry

If the tip of a blackberry cane is bent down and planted in the soil it will develop roots. These will give rise to a new shoot the following spring when the old cane can be severed close to the ground

Pruning and training

Post and wire support, (three strands – 60 cm (2 ft) apart) for training is best, the thornless varieties can be planted at 4 m (13 ft) apart,

48

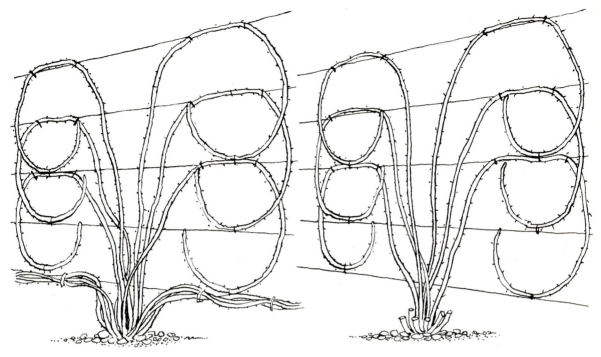

Pruning and training of blackberries
Left: Train the canes along horizontal support wires. As the new canes develop tie them to the bottom wire.
Right: Cut down the old canes after they have fruited and train the new canes along the wires

nearly double the distance would be advisable for Himalayan Giant. November is the time to plant, then in the following March cut the canes down to a good bud. New canes will soon develop, these should be tied to the wires for fruiting the next year.

Immediately after fruiting the old canes should be cut out and the strongest of the new canes tied in, I aim at keeping three each side of the plant. If the canes are longer than the space allows, loop them back towards the centre, any shortening necessary can be done the following February.

Care of rapidly growing new canes is important, I try to keep them out of the way of pickers feet by tying them progressively to the bottom wire.

Pests and diseases

I spray our blackberries with derris at blossom fall to control the raspberry beetle which can cause grubs to be found in the berries at picking time.

Varieties

Himalayan Giant: this was, at one time, the most commonly planted variety, it is extremely vigorous and terribly prickly. Unless controlled from the start it will soon take over a large area which can become virtually impenetrable. It is the heaviest cropper with a long season from August to October, the berries are medium size with quite a sharp taste. Not a variety I would recommend unless you enjoy handling thorny problems.

Merton Thornless: this was the first thornless variety I grew. It was raised at the John Innes Research Institute, and has now been largely superseded by Oregon Thornless an introduction from the United States.

The introduction of thornless varieties has made blackberries more manageable in small gardens and everything to do with growing them more pleasant.

Oregon Thornless: although found growing wild in Oregon in 1927 its introduction into

49

this country is fairly recent but in just a few years it has become the most popular variety. It crops well, the berries are a good size, they are sweet and the flavour is akin to our own native blackberries, its foliage is distinctive, with deep cuts in its leaves which give it a 'parsley' type foliage look.

It may not crop as heavy as the Himalayan Giant but you can plant it in half the space. Cropping time is from September to October.

Oregon Thornless, a variety with parsley-like foliage

Smoothstem and *Thornfree*: these are more recent thornless introductions, both raised at Beltsville Maryland, USA. According to report both are heavy croppers and with a vigorous fruiting season from late August to September.

Bedford Giant: this is an early cultivated blackberry. Its berries turn colour in July, they are sweet and juicy but the snag is that it is a vigorous and very prickly grower.

Boysenberries

I first grew boysenberries in 1939 when I was in Nottingham at the Lenton Research Station; its good qualities impressed me then and I still grow it.

The boysenberry was raised in California and is reported to be a cross involving not only a loganberry and a blackberry but also a raspberry. It differs somewhat from its near relative the youngberry, the berries turn red when starting to ripen before becoming dark purple when fully ripe. The berries are larger and more elongated than the youngberry.

Its growth behaviour is much like that of the loganberry and it responds to the same cultivations (see Loganberry p. 61) but could be more suitable than the loganberry for planting on light soils which are subject to seasonal drought conditions. I am surprised that it has taken so long for its virtues to be appreciated in this country. Plants of the thornless boysenberry are now generally available, the distance when planting should be 4 m (13 ft) and the best planting time is November.

Give a boysenberry a well-drained soil, a season to establish itself, a little attention such as removing of the old fruiting canes and tying in of the new ones (as with blackberries) and the result will be 3·6 to 4·5 kg (8 to 10 lb) of superb fruit per plant each August.

Cherries

However strong your desire to grow cherries may be, the first question to be answered is 'Can you protect the ripening crop against birds?' Without the possibility of complete protection against blackbirds in particular it is a waste of time contemplating the planting of either sweet or sour cherries. For this reason I would not recommend the planting of free-standing fruiting cherry trees in any garden;

however trained trees on a fence or wall that can be entirely netted are a totally different proposition. The recent introduction of Colt, a semi-dwarfing rootstock, is going to be a great help; its vigour is roughly comparable with that of MM 106 apple rootstock. On this new rootstock it should be easier to contain the trees in a fruitful condition within a limited area.

Care and cultivation

Cherries are more exacting than most fruit trees as far as soil conditions are concerned, good drainage is essential, a deep loam overlying chalk would be ideal. The trees blossom early, so districts subject to spring frosts and cold winds are less suitable unless some protection can be afforded. Warm conditions during the growing season produces the finest cherries, which to a large extent explains the reason for the concentration of commercial cherry growing in Kent. The best planting time is November, although two-year and sometime even four-year-old trees are recommended I prefer to start with a maiden (one-year old) and train it myself; if you do buy an older tree it should already be fan trained.

Prune fan-trained cherries in spring and summer to lessen the danger of entry of silver leaf disease. As sour cherries fruit on one-year-old wood, old wood should be cut back to encourage new growth. Also remove any weak or overcrowded shoots

In the absence of the ideal chalky subsoil, mix some garden lime with the filling soil and remember that routine application of garden lime may be needed every other year to keep the tree in full health.

Pruning and training

This can only be done by pruning and tying in the retained growths, this is a job that I do during the growing season when the risk of silver leaf and bacterial canker gaining entry is at its lowest level. Any large cut surfaces should be immediately painted over with bitumen paint or a proprietary wound paint. It is wise to go carefully with nitrogenous fertilisers otherwise wood growth could be excessive, but for good results potash (sulphate of potash) and phosphates (superphosphate) will be needed.

Many of the older varieties are either difficult to obtain or less suitable for training. Another problem concerns pollination, which is rather complex with cherries and makes the choice of varieties important. My choice would be as follows.

Varieties

SWEET CHERRIES

Merton Glory: a bright red cherry with creamy white flesh which is inclined to be soft but full of juice and flavour. Excellent pollinator for Early Rivers.

Early Rivers: very large fruit, deep crimson – black skin, reddish-black flesh, of good flavour when picked fully ripe in late June. Needs a suitable pollinator such as Merton Glory.

SOUR CHERRY

Morello: large deep-red to black fruit when ripe, self-fertile, can be planted with success on north-facing walls or fences. Ready middle of August.

Crab Apples

Whilst apple jelly can be made from cooking apples, for the finest flavoured jelly you really need good-flavoured crab apples. However, not all crab apple varieties make good jelly. We grow our crab apple trees in the ornamental garden, first to enjoy the blossom in the spring and then in the late summer the fruit crop follows.

Varieties

John Downie: probably the most popular choice, its white flowers in the spring are not spectacular but its bright orange-scarlet fruits have the flavour and qualities required to make good jelly.

Montreal Beauty: this has an upright habit and its large white, scented flowers tinged with pink, followed by huge orange-scarlet fruit is ideal for the smaller garden.

Red Glow: this makes a strong growing tree, salmon pink to scarlet flowers, the fruit is a good size.

Some of the small fruit varieties including Golden Hornet, Hopa, Red and Yellow Siberian also make excellent jelly.

Currants (Black)

Blackcurrants need good growing conditions and are a valuable source of vitamin C.

Care and cultivation

They need a well-drained fertile soil, preferably a deep medium to light loam supplied with liberal dressings of well-rotted compost or manure. It is essential to start with clean healthy stock, I insist on one-year-old plants that have been certified as virus free by the Ministry of Agriculture. To plant blackcurrants of dubious health is certainly foolish, troubles such as big bud reversion are so rife in private gardens that accepting a gift of cuttings may save some money but you acquire trouble and may be very disappointed as the cropping years progress.

Propagation of really healthy stock is easy, hard wood cuttings of the current season's growth, taken in the autumn, should be about 23 cm (9 in) long after the top 5 cm (2 in) has been taken off.

The more thoroughly the ground is prepared before planting blackcurrants the better and the best planting time is November. It is a mistake to crowd the plants, for good results 1·5 m (5 ft) spacing in the row is needed with 2·25 m (7 ft) between rows. This may look very generous at planting time but not so two years later.

To keep up the flow of strong growth in fruiting bushes it is necessary to apply either a balanced fertiliser such as Growmore, nitrochalk or sulphate of ammonia at the end of February. Thin mulches of well-rotted compost or manure are a great help applied in the spring when the top soil is moist; never starve blackcurrants.

Pruning

Many blackcurrant bushes are spoiled for life in their first season; do not make the common mistake with yours; cut each shoot down to two buds the following March, you will get no fruit that year but strong new growth will be built up for the first fruiting season and the bush will be made for life.

As blackcurrants fruit best on the previous year's wood it is essential to prune after fruiting to maintain the vitality of the bush and prevent overcrowding of the branches. I select the strongest of the new growths, removing the weaker shoots and as much of the old wood as possible.

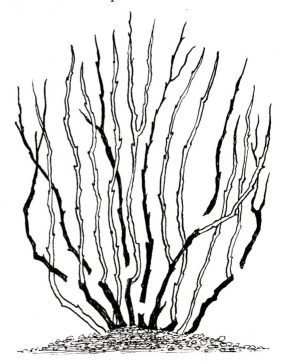

Blackcurrants produce fruit on one-year-old wood, so prune out the old wood to concentrate the plant's energies into fruit production

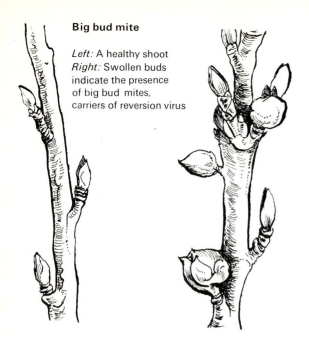

Big bud mite

Left: A healthy shoot
Right: Swollen buds
indicate the presence
of big bud mites,
carriers of reversion virus

Currants (Red and White)

Unlike blackcurrants they are not too fussy, they do well on most soils providing the

Pests and diseases

Big bud mite and reversion go hand in hand and preventive spraying with lime sulphur (not on those varieties that are sulphur sensitive) at the 10-pence-piece leaf-size stage is generally recommended but care is needed as many varieties are sensitive to lime sulphur and liable to suffer considerable leaf scorch.

Varieties

Baldwin: this is a well-proven late variety, it crops well, its compact growth habit makes it a good choice. The fruit has the highest vitamin C content. It is not lime sulphur sensitive.

Boskoop Giant: an early large-berried variety, good cropper makes a spreading type of bush.

Laxton's Giant: an early variety suitable for the exhibitor, very vigorous grower.

Jet: a recent introduction, late flowering so it escapes late spring frost damage when other varieties suffer badly. Its different flavour may not be appreciated by all.

Wellington XXX: a mid-season reliable cropper, vigorous grower, making a spreading type of bush unless corrected by pruning. Somewhat sensitive to lime sulphur.

Red- and whitecurrants fruit on spurs growing on the old wood unlike blackcurrants. Prune back laterals to two buds to establish fruiting spurs and thin out congested growth in the centre of the bush. The leaders should also be shortened.

54

drainage is good. Both fruit on the old wood (not the new wood as is the case with blackcurrants) so they can be grown as cordons, taking up little space. They do not require the generous compost or manurial treatments, a spring application of Growmore fertiliser will supply the potash which is important. Whether grown as cordons or as bushes, netting against birds at fruit ripening time is essential. Propagation from hardwood cuttings can be started in the autumn.

Varieties

Laxton's No 1: an early strong upright grower, good cropper, large bright red berries.

Red Lake: a mid-season cropper, good grower with an upright habit, large red berries.

White Versailles: an early cropper, good grower, the berries are large; the best white variety.

Damsons

Left: Unpruned bush
Above: Same bush after pruning

These are in fact members of the plum family. The true damson has a unique flavour and is highly regarded on that account for jam making. In recent years a much larger damson (Merryweather damson) has often been supplied to orders which simply requested a damson tree. It is more like a plum as not only does it lack the real blue-black colour but its skin is thicker and the flesh is a greenish yellow and lacking the full damson flavour; it is however a heavy cropper.

My farm is in the heart of the damson country with the Shropshire damson trees growing in many of the hedgerows. The fruit is small, it is a moderate cropper but seldom fails, so I can only conclude that the blossom is less susceptible to spring-frost damage than most of the plums.

The Shropshire damson makes a small tree; no routine pruning is needed, only the removal of dead wood as and when it occurs. Damson aphis is the chief pest and this can be controlled by winter spraying with a tar-distillate product during the fully dormant period between November and February.

On acid soils the addition of a little garden lime at planting time, followed by an overall application every other year, will help to maintain the health of the tree and in later years the stoning of the fruit.

Figs

Figs are very easy to grow but far more difficult to crop regularly in this country where the climate and conditions generally are so different from those of their home lands in Asia.

Care and cultivation

In a greenhouse it is possible to provide environmental conditions for successful cropping, two or even three crops a year can then be harvested but with present-day greenhouse and heating costs it is not a practical proposition for the average home gardener. With a greenhouse available for the winter it is wiser to grow the figs in pots rather than plant in a greenhouse border, the pots can then stand outside during the growing season and enjoy the frost protection afforded by the greenhouse during the winter. A 25-cm (10-in) pot is large enough, the best compost for potting would be loam from an old turf stack with some old mortar rubble mixed in it. Firm the potting mixture with a rammer but do not make it so firm that drainage is impeded, repotting without unnecessary disturbance of the roots would be advisable every other year.

Figs have a considerable water requirement, so watering throughout the growing season will be important. The growth, while limited by the constriction of the roots in the pot, should be kept healthy, so an occasional liquid fertiliser feed will be needed.

Winter protection

Grown outside figs will need protection against frost in the winter, otherwise the over-wintering embryo figs are destroyed and worst still the younger fruiting wood may also be killed if the frosts are severe. In our district it is essential to provide the fig tree with a covering of bracken or some other open protective material. Even so we are more than delighted when we succeed in getting a few ripe figs the following summer, gardeners further south have more chances of success with figs outdoors. The warmer the situation the better the results are likely to be, our plant is fan-trained on a west-facing fence; I would have preferred to have had it facing due south.

Varieties

Brown Turkey: one of the best, if not the best variety for this country; even so its vigour is such that some restriction of root growth is needed otherwise it makes excessive growth and produces little fruit. We planted ours in a sunken 40 gallon barrel with holes in the bottom for drainage; a good compost filling with some garden lime mixed in it provided the growing medium.

Figs in late summer
The bottom two figs are almost ready for eating. The centre two figs will not ripen before the frosts come. Next year's figs can be seen at the tip of the shoot

Gooseberries

One of the easiest fruits to grow, and although a well-drained deep soil suits them best they do well on practically any type of soil provided the drainage is satisfactory and they are well cared for and not planted in a frost pocket.

Care and cultivation
Feeding is important and I make sure that our gooseberries get an application of Growmore fertiliser every March. Gooseberries are very sensitive to a potash deficiency, this shows up as a brown marginal leaf scorch and unless remedied develops until cropping almost ceases. Growmore fertiliser with its high potash content applied annually prevents this happening altogether.

On poor, light or gravelly soils the addition of plenty of well-rotted compost or manure before planting will help, followed later on by mulching.

Grown as bushes the planting distances should be 1·5 to 2 m (5 to 6 ft) each way, single-stem cordons need be little more than 30 cm (1 ft) apart. For me bush gooseberries must always be grown on a leg, without a stem of at least 15 cm (6 in) fruit picking and weed control can be a painful business. I always plant one-year-old bushes, there is nothing to be gained by planting older and more expensive plants. The best planting time is Novem-ber although bare-rooted gooseberries can be planted at any time during the dormant season.

Pruning
The shoots of newly-planted bushes should be pruned back in March to about 8 cm (3 in) to outward pointing buds; this means no fruit in the first year after planting.

Pruning to prevent overcrowding of branches in established bushes can be done immediately after fruiting. However, birds are a problem in most districts, therefore I would suggest waiting until February, even so I still net our gooseberries to make doubly sure that I am left with plenty of buds to start the season.

Gooseberries are borne on spurs on the older wood and on one-year-old wood. Prune back laterals to three buds to establish fruiting spurs. Leaders should be shortened and any weak or congested growth should be removed.
Top: Unpruned bush
Bottom: The same bush after pruning

There is no difficulty in growing goose-berries as cordons as fruits develop on the closely pruned fruiting spurs. In fact goose-berries respond well to any type of training, cordons with three or four stems can be very rewarding. For a north wall or fence a fan-trained gooseberry is very suitable. In this case new growths are systematically tied in to replace the old wood.

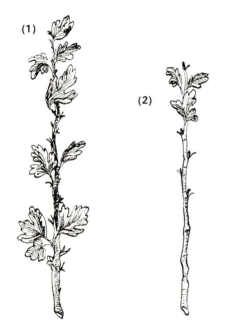

Preparing gooseberry cuttings
(1) A piece of current year's growth suitable for a cutting.
(2) Trim cutting to about 30 cm (1 ft) long and rub off all the buds except the top six. (3) Set the cuttings in a specially prepared trench, fill in with soil and firm

Propagation

Propagation is very easy; I take cuttings in late August, selecting strong new growths. For bushes I remove all except the top six buds, this is necessary to provide the clean stem. I plant the cuttings about 30 cm (1 ft) apart in a 20-cm-(8-in-) deep slit trench made with a spade and firm both sides, after planting, with my boot. By the following autumn the rooted one-year-olds are ready for planting out. The only difference in the preparation of cuttings for cordons concerns the removal of the buds, which in this case is limited to the part of the cutting below the ground.

Pests and diseases

The main pest problem is caused by goose-berry sawfly larvae which eat the leaves down to the skeletons. An application of derris insecticide deals effectively with them. Ameri-can gooseberry mildew disease attacks both foliage and berries. I spray with benomyl, both to protect and eradicate.

Varieties

Careless: the most popular garden variety, large green berries which cook well whilst still small. Good flavour when ripe.

Golden Drop: small dull-yellow berries with a really rich flavour, moderately vigorous grower, makes a compact bush. Subject to mildew.

Keepsake: early mid-season ripening, me-dium-sized green berries, makes a spreading-type bush.

Leveller: excellent-flavoured dessert variety, large-sized yellow-green berries, tends to be a weak grower on poor soils.

Whitesmith: an upright grower, large yellowish-green berries, very good flavour, heavy cropper.

Whinham's Industry: a vigorous upright grower, a good choice for heavy soils, dark-red berries, good flavour when ripe.

Grapes

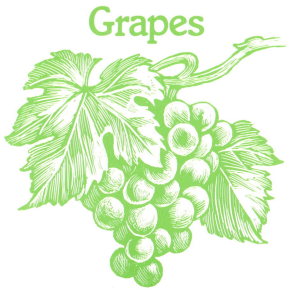

For growing grapes there are at least two requirements, space and some patience.

Care and cultivation

In one of our cold greenhouses I allocated a 3 m (10 ft) run for each of two vines. Having decided that heating was out of the question, I planted a Black Hamburg and a Buckland Sweetwater, the latter is less happy without heat. I then had to wait until the second summer before enjoying the first bunch of grapes. The vine was not allowed to form fruit in the first summer as this would have put too much strain on the young plant.

As the greenhouse is devoid of foundations I planted the one-year-old vines within the house in the autumn after having prepared the border by digging in some fish, blood and bone fertiliser. The greenhouse is equipped with horizontal supporting wires so it was not difficult to train two rods (stems) from buds at the top of each plant and I spaced these rods 1·25 m (4 ft) apart.

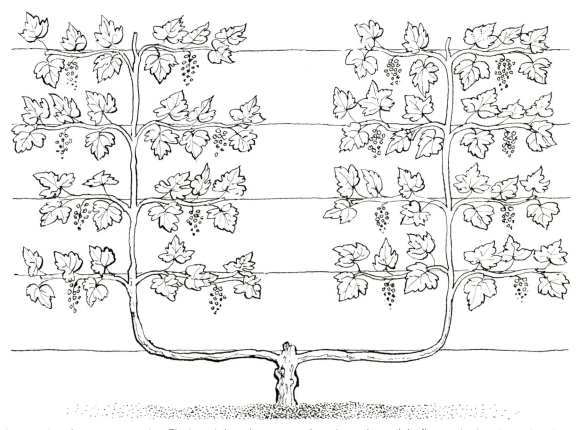

A grape vine after summer pruning. The laterals have been stopped two leaves beyond the flowers. In the winter when the leaves have fallen the laterals are cut back to the rod

To start the vine into growth in the spring the ventilation must be cut down to increase the temperature inside the greenhouse. Good ventilation is important when the vine is flowering and again when the pips are being formed. During the summer weather I keep the vines well watered but am careful not to over-water them. In very hot weather it is advisable to syringe the vines and damp down the greenhouse path each day to keep the atmosphere damp.

Thinning a bunch of young grapes

Pruning and training

At the end of the first season, just as the leaves began to fall, I shortened each rod to one third of its length, then in the following autumn to two thirds of its length and any side growths (laterals) were cut back to the rod. After that the rods were established over the roof of the house and little shortening was needed. A golden rule to remember is never to cut back into old wood during the growing season otherwise non-stop bleeding will occur.

Pruning in summer mostly consists of pinching out and stopping laterals. These develop rapidly and usually in excessive numbers; only one is needed on each side of a rod at each horizontal wire approximately 38 cm (15 in) apart. Each lateral is trained by carefully tying in onto the wires. The lateral is trained along the wires until it bears a bunch of flowers, then it is stopped two leaves beyond this point. Other side growths growing from the laterals are stopped at one leaf.

As the bunches of young fruits develop they will need to be thinned. About half the fruits from each bunch must be removed, mainly from the centre of the bunch. Great care must be taken not to bruise any of the young grapes. It may be necessary to thin the bunch again later in the season if its growth is looking congested. But the final large luscious fruits will make this worthwhile.

At the end of each season I cut the laterals back to the rods which I untie and lower from the training wires during the winter. I keep the greenhouse door open to let the cold in so preventing premature bud break.

Lowering the rods in the winter

Varieties

Black Hamburg: large black fruits. A hardy general purpose grape.

Buckland Sweetwater: a small white sweet grape.

Loganberries

The original Loganberry was thorned and according to reports was a cross between a blackberry and a raspberry which occurred in Oregon USA. The thorned version is still around but I prefer the now more popular thornless loganberry, which is a good cropper, the berries are just as large and no different in flavour or quality.

Care and cultivation

Loganberries need a considerable amount of space for the accommodation of their 2 m (6 ft) or even longer fruiting canes and a post and wire fence is ideal for the training and support of the canes. I allow each plant 2 m (6 ft) on either side, which means planting 4 m (12 ft) apart when growing more than one plant. Posts 1·5 m (5 ft) above ground with 3 strands of round wire provide adequate support.

The best time for planting is November, the ground should be well prepared, some well-rotted compost incorporated a few months before would be all to the good. The land must drain well as loganberries will not tolerate waterlogging.

There are a few golden rules for growing loganberries and the following is my recipe: never break the feeding roots, rely on surface hoeing and never dig near the base of the plants, give an annual spring mulch of well-rotted compost plus an application of blood, fish and bone fertiliser.

Pruning and training

In the first growing season the canes should be cut back in March almost to the ground, which means no fruit in their first year, in the following seasons the plants will carry both fruiting canes and new young canes at the same time. The old fruiting canes are cut out at ground level immediately after fruiting has finished, in the meantime I tie our young canes up to long vertical canes in order to prevent them getting damaged during the fruit picking period.

With old canes removed I select six of the strongest young canes for tying to the wires, three canes on each side are sufficient, the surplus canes I cut out without delay.

Pests and diseases

Loganberries are sometimes visited by the raspberry beetle which results in a maggot in the berries and a derris insecticide application at the petal-fall stage is the answer.

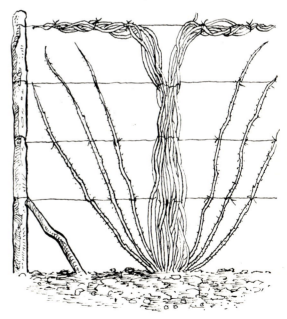

Training loganberries
The fruiting canes are trained in a fan-shaped arrangement while the new growths are tied in a bundle out of the way in the centre

Medlars

Melons

Medlars can be grown in almost any soil provided the drainage is satisfactory. It is usual to grow them as a half-standard or full-standard tree. The fruit is not particularly interesting, being hard and inedible when ready for picking at the end of October or later. Ripening occurs about two or three weeks later, this is quickly followed by further softening of the fruit before decay sets in. The variety we planted and subsequently grubbed out was Nottingham, it made a good-looking tree but we did not acquire a taste for its fruit.

The present high cost of greenhouse heating has practically eliminated melon growing as we knew it years ago, fortunately the introduction of varieties less dependent upon precise high temperature regimes has opened up greater possibilities for growing melons in frames or cold greenhouses. Even so the success with melons grown without heat varies considerably from season to season, the best results being obtained when both the spring and summer are warm and sunny.

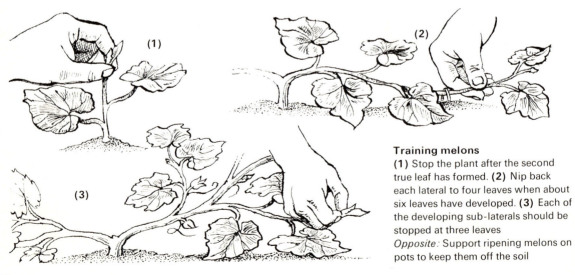

Training melons
(1) Stop the plant after the second true leaf has formed. **(2)** Nip back each lateral to four leaves when about six leaves have developed. **(3)** Each of the developing sub-laterals should be stopped at three leaves
Opposite: Support ripening melons on pots to keep them off the soil

Care and cultivation

In April I sow a single seed on edge in small peat pots filled with a peat-based seed compost and water them in. Then I put the pots into a small economic electric propagating frame on the greenhouse bench. Germination only takes a few days in a temperature of 18° to 21°C (65° to 70°F).

Once the seedlings begin to show their first true leaves I pot them on into 9-cm (3½-in) pots using a peat-based potting compost, to keep them growing well the temperature should not drop below 16°C (60°F).

I have found that planting before the end of May is unwise, as often the night temperatures are too low and the plants then receive a check to growth. More recently I have used peat growing bags, two plants to a bag and the bag placed at the high end of the frame. A bag is just about the width of a standard frame light, however, if available, a mound of old stacked turf makes an excellent growing medium for melons. The melon should be planted on a little mound above the level of either the peat or old turf in order that no water can possibly collect around the stem as this can cause the stem to rot.

Watering with care is a golden rule and the same applies to feeding, I use a liquid tomato fertiliser but only once a fortnight. Over-feeding produces excess foliage at the expense of fruit set.

Training and pollinating

When the second true leaf has formed the growing point should be pinched out to allow two laterals to develop. When these laterals have about six leaves they should be stopped at the fourth leaf to produce sub-laterals, which in turn should be stopped at the third leaf. The female flowers develop on these sub-laterals. I try to wait until a plant has five or six female flowers before pollinating, then when the day temperature is at its highest (about midday) I gently touch the inside centres of one or two wide open male flowers with a soft camel hair

Opposite: Luscious redcurrants (see page 54)

Pollinating melons
Top: Take some pollen off a male flower with a soft paintbrush

Bottom: Transfer the pollen to the stigma of the female flower (distinguishable by the large swelling behind the petals)

brush and then transfer the pollen on the brush onto the centre of the female flowers. To differentiate between the flowers, one looks at the back; female flowers have a small bulbous swelling behind them whereas the male flowers have none. I am satisfied if I can get four melons to set on a plant and it is important that they should set at the same time, otherwise the sizes will be very uneven.

I give frame melons ventilation, usually by sliding the light down about 10 cm (4 in) each morning and then closing up the frame in the early evening. In very hot weather it is advisable to shade the glass. When the melons start to ripen the aroma when the frame is opened is the warning to reduce the watering otherwise fruit cracking can occur.

Varieties

Charantais: small, orange flesh, delicious flavour.

Ogen: green flesh, round melon, needs a warm summer to build up its flavour.

Sweetheart (F₁ Hybrid): scarlet flesh, excellent flavour, tolerates low temperatures better than any other variety.

Nuts

The wild hazelnut is widely distributed throughout the country and wherever it grows the cultivated varieties can be planted with confidence.

Care and cultivation

Nuts are not exacting in their soil requirements as they will thrive on practically all types, from stiffish clay to light sand and they are not concerned about whether the soil is acid or alkaline. On rich soils they may tend to need more pruning but even so they will in addition to making a lot of wood growth, crop well.

Here at Clack's Farm we inherited a few old trees of the variety Cosford. Two of these we have kept and they now provide a shady entrance to our ornamental garden. In a good year the trees are heavily laden. It is then that we have to compete with the grey squirrels who bury the nuts anywhere and everywhere.

Two good cultivated varieties for garden planting are Cosford and Kentish Cob. The most popular of the two is Kentish Cob, which is rather misleadingly named, as it is a filbert nut. Both take a few years to settle down after planting before producing a crop of nuts, whilst hazelnuts and Cosford cobs are self-fertile the Kentish Cob needs the companionship of another variety for pollination purposes, Cosford would be a good choice.

Pruning

All nut trees tend to make a lot of new wood growth within the framework of the tree and unless some of this is pruned overcrowding of the branches develops. For good cropping results and the largest nuts it is best to treat each branch as a cordon.

Our old trees are on 60 cm (2 ft) clean stems, each year large numbers of buds develop on the trunks which we rub out, otherwise the trees would become enmeshed in a forest of new growth.

Varieties

Cosford: cob-shaped nuts with very sweet kernels.

Kentish Cob: very large and longish in shape, covered with a husk.

Walnuts: trees that crop are usually inherited, seldom is it possible to plant and crop a tree within a lifetime. Varieties such as Leeds Castle, Lady Irene or Northdown Clawnut can be planted but it would be a wait of at least twenty years before the first few nuts are likely to appear.

A well-pruned nut tree with an open centre

Peaches and Nectarines

The difference between peaches and nectarines concerns skin texture and flavour, peaches have a furry skin and nectarines a smooth one, but the growing technique is identical.

Care and cultivation

Peaches and nectarines are quite hardy in this country but with blossom time sometimes as early as late February, protection against spring frosts is always necessary for trees growing outside. After fruit set and onwards to the ripe-fruit stage, warm growing conditions are essential for complete success. An unheated greenhouse goes a long way to providing the protected conditions but in my experience it is wise to have some form of heating on hand to prevent the night temperatures falling below 0°C (32°F) from blossom time onwards.

A south- or west-facing fence or wall gives protection and some extra warmth which makes all the difference in outdoor peach growing but the protection acts as an umbrella so watering during the growing season is often necessary. Free-standing trees are a doubtful proposition in this country, fan-trained trees both inside the greenhouse and outside are best. These can be purchased as two- or three-year-old trees, trained initially in the nursery.

Late October or early November is the best planting time and a well-drained soil is essential. In a greenhouse it used to be common practice to dig out the border to a depth of 1 m (3 ft) and then make a compacted 15 cm (6 in) thick foundation of chalk with land drains above it. I have never embarked on preparations so elaborate but the solid chalk did prevent the development of a strong tap root and the resultant problem of strong growths above ground.

A good growing medium is a heavy loam made from old-rotted turf, I would like to add old mortar rubble to it but both are difficult to come by, so recently before planting I had to settle for a thorough cultivation of the existing soil plus a liberal dressing of garden lime worked in at the same time. Peaches need lime in the soil, not only for general health but for stone formation in the fruit as well. As with other fruit I give peaches an application of Growmore fertiliser in late February or early March, at which time I check the soil for acidity and apply garden lime if need be. Before planting the horizontal support wiring should be in position. I like to have the wires about 25 cm (10 in) apart. Immediately after planting firmly at the same depth as the tree was growing in the nursery (the depth mark will be seen on the stem), tie the branches carefully to the wires using raffia, always allowing room for the branches to expand within the tie.

Pruning and training

When the leaf buds break training commences, the buds for building up the fan are those on the upper sides of the young branches, the rest, those breaking downwards, inwards or outwards are rubbed out whilst still small with finger and thumb. The aim is to distribute evenly the young growths within the expanding fan, it may sometimes be necessary to remove some to prevent overcrowding. When fruiting commences in the second season spacing the young peaches at about 25 to 30 cm (10 to 12 in) apart will produce larger fruit. Any leaves that shade the individual fruits should be removed to prevent

67

uneven colouring.

There is always a tendency for strong upward-growing branches to develop in established trees, these should be completely removed, a slight V in the centre of the fan is an advantage.

Pests and diseases

As peach leaf curl is an ever present risk outside, I immediately spray newly planted dormant trees with a copper fungicide and make a rule to repeat the application each season just before blossoming and again in November.

Pests include aphids and red spider mite against which I spray with malathion, dryness at the roots increases the red spider mite problem.

Peach leaf curl causes blistering and distortion of the foliage

Varieties

PEACHES

Peregrine : the most reliable variety (August), excellent flavour.

Rochester : good cropper (August), fair flavour.

Duke of York : large fruit (July) excellent flavour.

NECTARINES

Early Rivers : large fruit (July) excellent flavour.

Pears

It is not difficult to grow a pear tree, a well-drained deep soil capable of holding moisture during dry periods would suit it well; but then comes the question 'Will it fruit in my garden?' Some of the older varieties of stewing pears will do well up north but dessert varieties need the warmth and the longer summer of the south east, so if they are to be planted in the cooler areas some form of protection is advisable. The oft quoted demarcation line south of the rivers Trent and Severn is about right, further north the overall climate changes quickly and up there dessert pears are best grown as trained trees on a south- or west-facing fence or wall.

Care and cultivation

Pears appreciate a warm sunny growing season but hate exposure to strongs winds which can seriously damage the foliage and young fruitlets.

In the past pears were generally grown as standard trees grafted or budded on pear seedling stock, they then made large trees and took years to come into bearing. Bush trees budded on quince rootstocks are now generally available and these can be expected to start fruiting within two or three years of planting.

Bush trees budded on Quince C rootstock can be planted 4 m (13 ft) apart, and will need staking throughout their lives. On the more vigorous Quince A rootstock it is better to allow 5 m (18 ft) between the trees. One point to note is that pears blossom early and are very susceptible to spring-frost damage, so planting in low-lying areas can be disappointing.

With a few exceptions such as Conference and Improved Fertility, most varieties need at least one and sometimes two other varieties which flower at the same time to be planted alongside them for pollination purposes. Pears do best when the ground around them is clean cultivated, an application of Growmore fertiliser in late February or early March will keep the trees in good health.

In seasons when the fruit set is heavy it may be advisable to do some hand thinning but not until after the fruitlets have definitely set and the tree has shed naturally its unwanted extras, which could well be more than half of the original fruit set.

Harvesting and storing

Pears should be gathered before they are fully ripe but not before they are mature, in other words wait until the fruit stalk parts easily from the spur, a slight lifting of the pear will indicate whether or not picking should begin, it may be that all the pears on the tree will not be ready at the same time.

Great care is needed to avoid bruising, in store pears need watching daily if you are to enjoy them at their best.

Pests and diseases

Pear scab can be a problem, I start spraying with captan at bud break, with repeats at green bud, white bud and petal fall (see page 32). After that if the season is damp and warm two or three further sprays at fortnightly intervals are advisable.

Varieties

Beurré Hardy: inclined to be a vigorous grower, a heavy cropper, fruit large and rather uneven in shape, skin greenish yellow with russeted patches, flushed with a trace of red. Flesh tender and juicy, excellent flavour, at its best in October. Mid-season flowering.

Catillac: vigorous grower, heavy cropper, large roundish fruit, probably the best cooking pear which keeps well during its season, December to April. Late flowering.

Conference

Conference: a fairly vigorous grower, the most reliable cropper, will succeed planted on its own. Medium sized fruit with longish neck. Dark green russeted skin, when fully ripe very juicy and sweet. The number one garden pear. Season October to November. Mid-season flowering.

Doyenné du Comice: moderate grower, only fair cropper, needs good pollinators such as Beurré Hardy or Glou Morceau. Well grown the fruit is large with pale-yellow russeted skin. Our finest pear for flavour and quality, not one of the easiest to grow. Season November. Late flowering.

Fertility: an upright grower with moderate vigour, dull-yellow russeted skin, fruit juicy but lacks flavour. Season October. Mid-season flowering.

Glou Morceau: makes a spreading tree, with moderate vigour, skin green turning to yellow on ripening. A variety with a delicious flavour but for the warmer climates only. Season December to January. Late flowering.

Louise Bonne de Jersey: this makes an upright grower, well suited for the small garden, fruit medium size, skin is yellowish-green flushed with red and red spots, flesh tender, flavour excellent. Regular cropper when planted with a suitable pollinator such as Conference. Season October. Early flowering.

Nouveau Poiteau: an upright grower but inclined to spread, fair cropper, fruit large with greenish-yellow skin covered with a reddish russet. Tender flesh, good flavour. Season November. Late flowering.

Onward: a new variety of considerable promise, moderate growth, fruit shape and colour not unlike Comice, one of its parents. Flavour excellent. Season early September. Late flowering.

Packham's Triumph: a fairly vigorous grower, fruit mainly large but variable in size and shape. When ripe, skin is bright yellow with some russeting. Very juicy, good flavour. A good cropper. Season November/December. Early flowering.

Williams' Bon Chrétien: this is probably the best known pear in the world, either as Williams' or its other name Bartlett. Vigorous grower, free cropper, medium-size fruit, golden-yellow skin with russet spots and faint red streaks when ripe. Tender flesh, full of juice, excellent flavour. Must be picked before the fruit turn yellow otherwise the flesh is dry and lacking in flavour. Season September. Mid-season flowering.

Winter Nellis: a one time popular variety, makes a tree of moderate vigour, fruit inclined to be small. When ripe the skin is yellow with dark spots. Sweet, juicy and full of flavour, an excellent keeping pear. Season November to January. Late flowering.

Pollination Table for Pears

Early flowering	Mid-season flowering	Late flowering
Duchesse d'Angouléme	Beurré Hardy	Catillac (T)
Easter Beurré	Baurré Superfin	Clapp's Favourite
Emile d'Heyst	Conference	Doyenné du Comice
Louise Bonne de Jersey	Doyenné Boussoch (T)	Glou Morceau
Packham's Triumph	Durondeau	Gorham
	Fertility	Improved Fertility
	Jargonelle (T)	Marie Louise
	Joséphine de Malines	Nouveau Poiteau
	Merton Pride (T)	Onward
	Triomphe de Vienne	Pitmaston Duchess (T)
	Williams' Bon Crétien	Winter Nelis

T – triploid, needs two pollinators

Plums

Plums are the most hardy of all our stone tree fruits.

Care and cultivation

Provided the drainage is satisfactory medium to heavy soils are best for plums, on light soils subject to drying out during the summer artificial watering may be required to swell the fruit and prevent it shrivelling rather than ripening.

In common with all stone fruits periodical applications of garden lime will be necessary except on soils which are naturally very calcareous. In the absence of sufficient available calcium in the soil, fruit drop at stoning time can be almost complete; additionally too low a calcium level affects the overall health of the tree.

I have found from experience that plums do not like their root areas covered with grass or weeds, clean cultivation under the trees is therefore best.

Pruning

In the first two or three years after planting plum trees tend to make a lot of strong wood growth but after that they settle down to produce fruiting wood. Unless absolutely necessary I do not prune free-standing plum trees but crossing and dead branches can be cut out in May when growth is active. It is wise to paint over any saw cuts with a wound or bitumen paint to prevent entry of silver leaf disease.

Pests and diseases

Plums are less subject to insect pests and diseases than either apples or pears, however in many districts bullfinch damage in the spring when the fruit buds start to swell can be a serious problem.

On account of the bullfinches I have gone over to growing fan-trained plums on fences. The plums do object to the necessary pruning which needs to be done with care, but now this does mean that we can net the trees early in the year and we do get some superb quality plums.

Silver leaf is a disease caused by a fungus which attacks quite a number of trees especially plums. Whilst as a result of the disease the leaves have a silvery appearance the fungus is actually in the wood, affected branches when cut through show a dark brown or black stain. Silver leaf kills and is very infectious, the Silver Leaf Order of 1923 requires the removal and burning of infected dead wood before the 15th July. Infected dead wood left about to get damp produces the fungus fructifications which spread the disease far

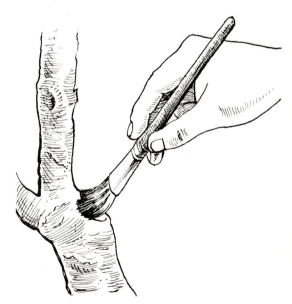

Paint over pruning cuts with bitumen

and wide in the area. All wounds on plum trees, whether caused by pruning or gale damage should be painted over immediately with a wound or bitumen paint. Poor growing conditions increase the risk of silver leaf, I give our plums a Growmore fertiliser application towards the end of February.

Varieties

Cambridge Gage: a rather small yellowish-green plum, a fairly free cropper for one with a gage flavour. Ripe August/September.

Coe's Golden Drop: medium sized, amber-yellow dotted with red, good flavour. At its best when grown in a warm situation. Ripe September/October.

Green Gage: the true gage, olive green with slight red flush and spots, delicious flavour but not a reliable cropper. Ripe late August.

Jefferson: large golden plum flushed and spotted with red plus some russet patches. Excellent flavour, juicy and sweet. Quite a good cropper. Ripe September.

Kirke's: medium to large plum, purple covered with blue bloom. Superb flavour, juicy and sweet. Best grown on a warm wall. Ripe September.

Rivers Early Prolific: a small, early, blue plum, excellent for cooking. Ripe July.

Transparent Gage: medium sized, golden-yellow plum slightly flushed with violet. Tender flesh, sweet aromatic flavour. Best grown against a wall.

Victoria: large bright red with darker spots when fully ripe. Sweet, moderate dessert flavour, cooks well. The variety for the single tree grower as it is self-fertile. Ripe August early September.

Pollination Table for Plums

Early flowering	Mid-season flowering	Late flowering
Self fertile		
Denniston's Superb	Czar	Belle de Louvain
Monarch	Laxton's Gage	Bradley's King Damson
Warwickshire Drooper	Merryweather Damson	Giant Prune
	Pershore	Shropshire Damson
	Purple Pershore	
	Severn Cross	
	Victoria	
Require cross pollination		
Coe's Golden Drop	Early Laxton	Blaisdon Red
Farleigh Damson	Kirke's Blue	Cambridge Gage
Golden Transparent	Purple Gage	Cox's Emperor
Jefferson Gage	Transparent Gage	Early Transparent
President		Frogmore Damson
River's Early Prolific		Green Gage
		Late Transparent
		Marjorie's Seedling
		Oullin's Golden Gage
		Pond's Seedling
		Red Magnum Bonum
		Wyedale

Quinces

Raspberries

In addition to their more common use as rootstocks for propagating pears, quinces are useful as a fruit, especially for jelly making. Like pears they dislike cold winds and are not for planting in northern districts, but in the south given a fairly moist deep soil quinces can be grown either as a bush or a half-standard tree. The fruit does not ripen until late October. After picking it should not be stored close to either apples or pears as its strong aroma is liable to affect their flavour.

The variety we grow is Vranja, which is self-fertile, the only pruning needed is the cutting out of overcrowded branches.

Autumn-fruiting raspberries are pruned down to ground level in February

Raspberries are a fairly simple fruit to grow and are suitable for both freezing and jam making.

Care and cultivation

The fact that the wild raspberry grows in abundance in the west of Scotland gives a clear indication of the soil and climatic conditions that suit it best. The same conditions suit the cultivated varieties, a medium soil well drained but never short of moisture is ideal as a district with a cool summer. On a light soil with a tendency to dry out quickly an addition of some organic matter, such as well-rotted compost or peat, to improve the moisture-holding capacity is advisable; an application of bonemeal is always a good way to improve the fertility of a poor soil.

Before planting raspberries the ground should be well prepared, deeply dug and free from perennial weeds and their roots. Otherwise keeping the canes free from serious weed competition later on becomes a great problem, siting is less important, raspberries prefer full sun but will crop in partial shade.

With raspberries so prone to virus diseases it is prudent to start with healthy young canes carrying a Ministry of Agriculture certificate of health, on no account start with canes dug from a fruiting row.

73

The best time for planting is November, this allows the canes to make new roots well ahead of the active growing season. I plant the young canes 45 cm (18 in) apart in the row, making sure that each one is planted firmly, and when planting more than one row I allow at least 2 m (6 ft) between the rows. The following March I check each plant to see it is firm, as frosts may have lifted the roots of some slightly, this is also the time to cut down the newly planted canes to 15 cm (6 in) above ground. With summer-fruiting varieties it means no fruit in the first season but with autumn-fruiting varieties the new young canes thrown up during the summer will fruit and should be allowed to do so.

At no time should the ground near raspberries be cultivated deeply, this is a frequent cause of deterioration in health and cropping; I use a Dutch hoe for surface weed control.

Mulching with well-rotted compost or manure is excellent, a March application of Growmore fertiliser added to this is my routine treatment each year.

Training and pruning
For summer-fruiting varieties I erect the support posts and three strands of round wire before planting. I like the top wire at about 1·5 m (5 ft) with a spacing of 45 cm (18 in) between the other two. Autumn-fruiting canes only need support string or wire just

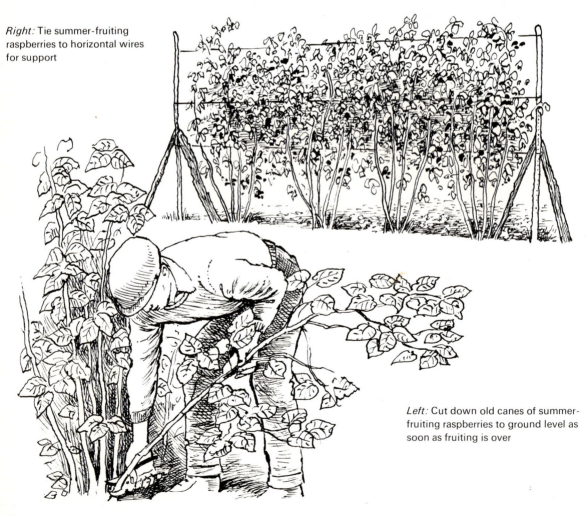

Right: Tie summer-fruiting raspberries to horizontal wires for support

Left: Cut down old canes of summer-fruiting raspberries to ground level as soon as fruiting is over

before fruiting to prevent the weight of fruit bowing the canes to the ground.

With established summer-fruiting varieties the old fruiting canes are cut out close to the ground as soon as possible after cropping has ended, the new young canes can then be tied in loosely with raffia to the wires. I select the five strongest of each plant and discard the weaker canes. If at the turn of the year some of the canes exceed 1·5 m (5 ft) I top them at that height.

Autumn-fruiting varieties are cut down to near ground level at the end of February each year to encourage the growth of young canes.

Pests and diseases

Raspberry beetle can be a troublesome pest. To prevent maggots in the fruit spray with derris at the white-flower-bud stage and repeat at petal fall. Don't spray when the bees are working the fully open blossom.

Varieties

SUMMER-FRUITING

Delight : very heavy cropper, berries are the size of loganberries but have a poor flavour.

Glen Clova : very vigorous new growths make picking very difficult, should be grown on its own; good flavour.

Malling Admiral : late season, large berries of poor flavour.

Malling Jewel : good cropper, keeps its berries clear of the foliage, excellent flavour.

Malling Promise : heavy cropper, rather soft berries of good flavour.

AUTUMN-FRUITING

Fall Gold : golden-yellow fruit, excellent flavour.

Heritage : erect canes, good cropper, good flavour.

September : a quality fruit for September and October; very good flavour.

Zeva : stout canes, large berries, good flavour.

Strawberries

It is not difficult to understand why commercial strawberry growing is located in certain areas, to crop really well the soil needs to be very fertile and well drained. In most gardens it is possible to create these growing conditions by careful and thorough pre-planting preparations of the ground.

Care and cultivation

Strawberries dislike chalky soils and seldom do well when the land is liable to dry out excessively in drought periods. Never plant strawberries in the shade, the sunny site selected for the planting should be clean and certainly free from perennial-weed roots as the bed may well stay down two or three years. Another point to consider is spring frost damage. With strawberries growing near the ground the risk of blossom damage is always greater than with bush or tree fruits. If there is a choice select the higher part of the garden, even if it is only fractionally higher the lowest temperatures will be registered elsewhere.

It matters little whether the soil is light, medium or heavy, it should be well dug to the full depth of a spade with a liberal amount of well-rotted compost or manure incorporated at the same time, if neither is available use granulated peat. If this can be done a month ahead of the planting so much the better.

It is important to start with healthy stock, plants that carry the Ministry of Agriculture's certificate showing that they have been inspected during the growing season and reported to be healthy and true to variety.

These plants are grown in isolation, and only by growing them in this way is it possible to maintain healthy plants for propagation. There is always a risk of virus problems when taking runner plants from a fruiting bed.

Planting and spacing

Planting can be done any time from August to March depending upon the weather and soil conditions. For summer-fruiting varieties I prefer to plant in August or, at the latest, September, this allows time for the plants to make a good root system before the soil gets cold. These early plantings give good crops of large fruit the following June and July. Later plantings may not be strong enough to fruit in the first season, in which case it is best to remove the blossom from the plants. Late-planted autumn-fruiting varieties can be cropped in the first year after de-blossoming them in May if need be. Pot-grown plants always get away more quickly, bare-rooted plants should have their roots moistened before planting.

For individual row plantings allow 38 cm (15 in) between the plants and 75 cm (30 in) between the rows, for double row beds I find 38 cm (15 in) between the plants and the rows with a 75 cm (30 in) path between each bed adequate. It is important to plant firmly with the crown just above ground level, if a crown is submerged it may rot and the plant subsequently dies.

The week or so after planting is critical, especially if the weather and soil conditions are dry, the plants should be watered to prevent them flaging. I make a point of checking young plants after a frosty spell, if they have lifted a little I firm the soil around them.

I give our plants, young as well as old ones, a feed with Growmore fertiliser early in March, this helps to make healthy growth the moment the soil and air conditions warm up.

Place straw round strawberry plants to prevent damage to fruits by soil being splashed onto them in wet weather

Black polythene can be laid as an alternative to straw to keep fruit clean

We like to spread our ripe strawberry season as wide as possible, by covering a few plants with cloches in March we can pick a month earlier from these than from the unprotected ones.

76

Without protection the summer-fruiting varieties will blossom in May. I wait as long as possible before putting either straw or thin black plastic film down under the flower trusses, as doing it increases the risk of the flowers being damaged by frost. When this happens the flowers develop black centres which means that the embryo strawberries have been killed.

Runners

At fruiting time the plants start sending out runners, which if left will root and make new plants. I like to keep the spaces between the rows or beds absolutely clean so I cut the runners off close to the parent plant as soon as possible.

Cut off runners close to the parent plant

Strawberry flowers with black centres due to frost damage

In a small garden it is only worthwhile converting runners into replacement plants if the parent plants are absolutely healthy but this is highly unlikely after the first fruiting season.

When fruiting has finished the straw or plastic film should be removed and the foliage cut off with a pair of shears and burnt. It is then time for a repeat application of Growmore fertiliser to supply the nutrients needed for new growth and to build up the crown for the following season's fruiting.

Varieties

SUMMER FRUITING

Cambridge Favourite: heavy cropper, moderate flavour, freezes well.

Domanil: late mid-season, heavy cropper, dark coloured berries, good flavour.

Gorella: heavy cropper, fair flavour, reasonable resistance to botrytis.

Red Gauntlet: heavy cropper, fair flavour, does well under cloches.

Royal Sovereign: this is the strawberry that I would like to grow for quality and flavour, it is still in a class by itself but its susceptibility to disease almost rules it out. However it is still the best for forcing, potted up in September and brought into a warm greenhouse at the end of February, the ripe strawberry season will begin in April.

Talisman: good cropper, good flavour, compact plant.

Tamella: good cropper, very good flavour, forces well and freezes well.

Tenira: late mid-season, very heavy cropper, excellent flavour.

AUTUMN FRUITING

Gento: will also have a small crop in summer, good autumn cropper, even crops on runner plants, excellent flavour.

Rabunda: heavy cropper, fruit brighter than Gento but not equal in flavour.

Worcester berries

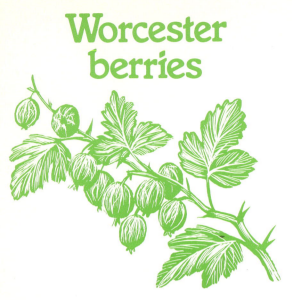

According to report this hybrid berry is the result of a cross between a gooseberry and a blackcurrant. Its growing habit closely resembles that of a gooseberry but in my experience the branches are more slender and certainly more thorny than gooseberries and this can make picking a painful business.

We grew it at one time mainly on account of its name rather than its fruit, which look like small gooseberries with a flavour that could be said to be in some way related to that of a ripe blackcurrant.

Youngberries

Another hybrid berry originating in the USA from a cross between a raspberry and a blackberry. With us it is an excellent cropper, the berries being freely produced in large clusters, they look very much like shiny blackberries but are somewhat larger and more juicy. The flavour is not unlike that of the blackberry but less sweet, more inclined to be slightly acid. We find them first class for jam making, and, in fact, for all the purposes blackberries are used for in the kitchen.

Care and cultivation
The youngberry is a strong grower without thorns, its long fruiting canes can exceed 3 m (10 ft) in length. We planted them 4 m (13 ft) apart, which was barely sufficient. Treated in the same manner as blackberries we found it capable of outcropping most varieties, it thrives in semi-shade if the soil conditions are moist and good. Planting is best done in November. Mulching in the late winter with well-rotted compost gives good results especially when followed by an application of fish, blood and bone fertiliser or Growmore fertiliser.

Training
The young canes should then be tied to the bottom support wire clear of the ground and cut down to a couple of inches of the ground the following March. The new growths that follow will be the fruiting wood for the following year; they should be kept loosely tied to the support wires as they grow.

Each year after fruiting the old wood should be cut out as soon as possible and the new young canes tied in to replace them. Like all cane fruits the youngberry is surface rooting, disturbance of the ground around the plants should be avoided, weed control is best done with a Dutch hoe.

Index